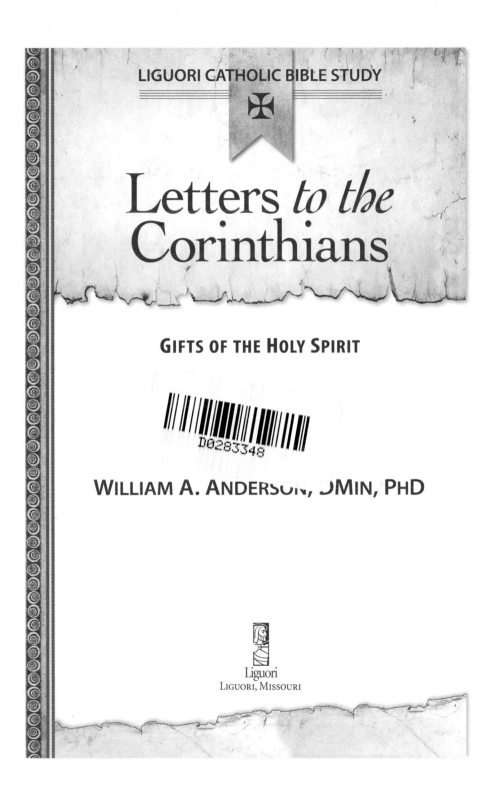

LIGUORI CATHOLIC BIBLE STUDY

Letters *to the* Corinthians

GIFTS OF THE HOLY SPIRIT

WILLIAM A. ANDERSON, DMIN, PHD

Liguori
LIGUORI, MISSOURI

Imprimi Potest: Harry Grile, CSsR, Provincial
Denver Province, The Redemptorists

Printed with Ecclesiastical Permission and Approved for Private or Instructional Use

Nihil Obstat: Rev. Msgr. Kevin Michael Quirk, JCD, JV
Censor Librorum

Imprimatur: + Michael J. Bransfield
Bishop of Wheeling-Charleston (West Virginia)
December 27, 2012

Published by Liguori Publications
Liguori, Missouri 63057

To order, call 800-325-9521
www.liguori.org

Library of Congress Cataloging-in-Publication Data
Anderson, William Angor, 1937-
    Letters to the Corinthians : gifts of the Holy Spirit / William A.
Anderson. — First edition
        pages cm
    1. Bible. Corinthians—Commentaries. 2. Bible. Corinthians—Study and
teaching. 3. Catholic Church—Doctrines. I. Title.
    BS2675.53.A53 2013
    227'.20071—dc23

                                                                2013006378

p ISBN: 978-0-7648-2126-4
e ISBN: 978-0-7648-6838-2

Liguori Publications, a nonprofit corporation, is an apostolate of the Redemptorists. To learn more about the Redemptorists, visit Redemptorists.com.

Printed in the United States of America
17 16 15 14 13 / 5 4 3 2 1
First Edition

Contents

Dedication 5

Acknowledgments 7

Introduction to *Liguori Catholic Bible Study* 9

***Lectio Divina* (Sacred Reading)** 11

How to Use This Bible-Study Companion 14
> *A Process for Sacred Reading* 15
> *Group-Study Formats* 16

Introduction: Letters to the Corinthians 19

Lesson 1   Condemnation of Disorders 26
> *Group Study (1 Corinthians 1—2)* 27

Lesson 2   Temples of the Holy Spirit 37
> *Part 1: Group Study (1 Corinthians 3—4)* 38
> *Part 2: Individual Study (1 Corinthians 5—7)* 45

Lesson 3   Offerings to Idols 55
> *Part 1: Group Study (1 Corinthians 8—9)* 56
> *Part 2: Individual Study (1 Corinthians 10—11)* 63

> NOTE: The length of each Bible section varies. Group leaders should combine sections as needed to fit the number of sessions in their program.

Lesson 4   Spiritual Gifts 74

Part 1: Group Study (1 Corinthians 12—14:19) 75

Part 2: Individual Study (1 Corinthians 14:20—16) 84

Lesson 5   Ministers of the New Covenant 96

Part 1: Group Study (2 Corinthians 1—3:6) 98

Part 2: Individual Study (2 Corinthians 3:7—5) 107

Lesson 6   An Acceptable Time 116

Part 1: Group Study (2 Corinthians 6—7) 117

Part 2: Individual Study (2 Corinthians 8—9) 122

Lesson 7   Boasting in the Lord 128

Part 1: Group Study (2 Corinthians 10—11:29) 129

Part 2: Individual Study (2 Corinthians 11:30—13) 134

About the Author 141

Dedication

This series is lovingly dedicated to the memory of my parents, Kathleen and Angor Anderson, in gratitude for all they shared with all who knew them, especially my siblings and me.

Acknowledgments

Bible studies and reflections depend on the help of others who read the manuscript and make suggestions. I am especially indebted to Sister Anne Francis Bartus, CSJ, DMin, whose vast experience and knowledge were very helpful in bringing this series to its final form.

Introduction to
Liguori Catholic Bible Study

READING THE BIBLE can be daunting. It's a complex book, and many a person of goodwill has tried to read the Bible and ended up putting it down in utter confusion. It helps to have a companion, and *Liguori Catholic Bible Study* is a solid one. Over the course of this series, you'll learn about biblical messages, themes, personalities, and events and understand how the books of the Bible rose out of the need to address new situations.

Across the centuries, people of faith have asked, "Where is God in this moment?" Millions of Catholics look to the Bible for encouragement in their journey of faith. Wisdom teaches us not to undertake Bible study alone, disconnected from the Church that was given Scripture to share and treasure. When used as a source of prayer and thoughtful reflection, the Bible comes alive.

Your choice of a Bible-study program should be dictated by what you want to get out of it. One goal of *Liguori Catholic Bible Study* is to give readers greater familiarity with the Bible's structure, themes, personalities, and message. But that's not enough. This program will also teach you to use Scripture in your prayer. God's message is as compelling and urgent today as ever, but we get only part of the message when it's memorized and stuck in our heads. It's meant for the entire person—physical, emotional, and spiritual.

We're baptized into life with Christ, and we're called to live more fully with Christ today as we practice the values of justice, peace, forgiveness, and community. God's new covenant was written on the hearts of the people of Israel; we, their spiritual descendants, are loved that intimately by God today. *Liguori Catholic Bible Study* will draw you closer to God, in whose image and likeness we are fashioned.

Group and Individual Study

The *Liguori Catholic Bible Study* series is intended for group and individual study and prayer. This series gives you the tools to start a study group. Gathering two or three people in a home or announcing the meeting of a Bible-study group in a parish or community can bring surprising results. Each lesson in this series contains a section to help groups study, reflect, pray, and share biblical reflections. Each lesson also has a second section for individual study.

Many people who want to learn more about the Bible don't know where to begin. This series gives them a place to start and helps them continue until they're familiar with all the books of the Bible.

Bible study can be a lifelong project, always enriching those who wish to be faithful to God's Word. When people complete a study of the whole Bible, they can begin again, making new discoveries with each new adventure into the Word of God.

Lectio Divina
(Sacred Reading)

BIBLE STUDY isn't just a matter of gaining intellectual knowledge of the Bible; it's also about gaining a greater understanding of God's love and concern for creation. The purpose of reading and knowing the Bible is to enrich our relationship with God. God loves us and gave us the Bible to illustrate that love. As Pope Benedict XVI reminded us, a study of the Bible is not only an intellectual pursuit but also a spiritual adventure that should influence our dealings with God and neighbor.

The Meaning of *Lectio Divina*

Lectio divina is a Latin expression that means "divine or sacred reading." The process for *lectio divina* consists of Scripture readings, reflection, and prayer. Many clergy, religious, and laity use *lectio divina* in their daily spiritual reading to develop a closer and more loving relationship with God. Learning about Scripture has as its purpose the living of its message, which demands a period of reflection on the Scripture passages.

Prayer and *Lectio Divina*

Prayer is a necessary element for the practice of *lectio divina*. The entire process of reading and reflecting is a prayer. It's not merely an intellectual pursuit; it's also a spiritual one. Before the introduction of the book of the Bible under consideration, this present text includes a prayer for gathering one's thoughts before moving on to the passages in each section. This prayer may be used privately or in a group. For those who use the book for daily spiritual reading, the prayer for each section may be repeated each day. Some may wish to keep a journal of each day's meditation.

Pondering the Word of God

Lectio divina is the ancient Christian spiritual practice of reading the holy Scriptures with intentionality and devotion. This practice helps Christians center themselves and descend to the level of the heart to enter an inner quiet space, finding God.

This sacred reading is distinct from reading for knowledge or information, and it's more than the pious practice of spiritual reading. It is the practice of opening ourselves to the action and inspiration of the Holy Spirit. As we intentionally focus on and become present to the inner meaning of the Scripture passage, the Holy Spirit enlightens our minds and hearts. We come to the text willing to be influenced by a deeper meaning that lies within the words and thoughts we ponder.

In this space, we open ourselves to be challenged and changed by the inner meaning we experience. We approach the text in a spirit of faith and obedience as a disciple ready to be taught by the Holy Spirit. As we savor the sacred text, we let go of our usual control of how we expect God to act in our lives and surrender our hearts and consciences to the flow of the divine (*divina*) through the reading (*lectio*).

The fundamental principle of *lectio divina* leads us to understand the profound mystery of the Incarnation, "The Word became flesh," not only in history but also within us.

Praying *Lectio* Today

Before you begin, relax your body and maintain a posture of prayer (back straight, eyes shut, feet flat on the floor). Then practice these four simple actions:

1. Read a passage from Scripture or the daily Mass readings. This is known as *lectio*. (If the Word of God is read aloud, the hearers listen attentively.)
2. Pray the selected passage with attention as you listen for a specific meaning that comes to mind. Once again, the reading is listened to or silently read and reflected or meditated on. This is known as *meditatio*.

3. The exercise becomes active. Pick a word, sentence, or idea that surfaces from your consideration of the chosen text. Does the reading remind you of a person, place, or experience? If so, pray about it. Compose your thoughts and reflection into a simple word or phrase. This prayer-thought will help you remove distractions during the *lectio*. This exercise is called *oratio*.

4. In silence, with your eyes closed, quiet yourself and become conscious of your breathing. Let your thoughts, feelings, and concerns fade as you consider the selected passage in the previous step (*oratio*). If you're distracted, use your prayer word to help you return to silence. This is *contemplatio*.

This exercise can take as long as you want, but in the context of this Bible study, 10 to 20 minutes should be sufficient.

Many teachers of prayer call contemplation the prayer of resting in God, a prelude to losing oneself in the presence of God. Scripture is transformed in our hearing as we pray and allow our hearts to unite intimately with the Lord. The Word truly takes on flesh, and this time it is manifested in our flesh.

How to Use This Bible-Study Companion

THE BIBLE, along with the commentaries and reflections found in this study, will help participants become familiar with the Scripture texts and lead them to reflect more deeply on the texts' message. At the end of this study, participants will have a firm grasp of the letters to the Corinthians and realize how those letters offer spiritual nourishment. This study is not only an intellectual adventure, it's also a spiritual one. The reflections lead participants into their own journey with the Scripture readings.

Context

When the author wrote his letters to the Corinthians, he was writing to a community with many gifts, but a community that needed guidance in the proper use of these gifts. To help readers learn about each passage in relation to those around it, each lesson begins with an overview that puts the Scripture passages into context.

Part 1: Group Study

To give participants a comprehensive study of Letters to the Corinthians, the book is divided into seven lessons. Lesson 1 is group study only; Lessons 2 through 7 are divided into Part 1, group study, and Part 2, individual study. For example, Lesson 2 covers passages from 1 Corinthians 3—7. The study group reads and discusses only 1 Corinthians 3—4 (Part 1). Participants privately read and reflect on 1 Corinthians 5—7 (Part 2).

Group study may or may not include *lectio divina*. With *lectio divina*, the group meets for ninety minutes using the first format on page 16. Without *lectio divina*, the group meets for one hour using the second format on page 16, and participants are urged to privately read the *lectio divina* section at the end of Part 1. It contains additional reflections on the Scripture passages studied during the group session that will take participants even further into the passages.

Part 2: Individual Study

The passages not covered in Part 1 are divided into three to four shorter components, one to be studied each day. Participants who don't belong to a study group can use the lessons for private sacred reading. They may choose to reflect on one Scripture passage per day, making it possible for a clearer understanding of the Scripture passages used in their *lectio divina* (sacred reading).

A PROCESS FOR SACRED READING

Liguori Publications has designed this study to be user friendly and manageable. However, group dynamics and leaders vary. We're not trying to keep the Holy Spirit from working in your midst, thus we suggest you decide beforehand which format works best for your group. If you have limited time, you could study the Bible as a group and save prayer and reflection for personal time.

However, if your group wishes to digest and feast on sacred Scripture through both prayer and study, we recommend you spend closer to ninety minutes each week by gathering to study and pray with Scripture. *Lectio divina* (see page 11) is an ancient contemplative prayer form that moves readers from the head to the heart in meeting the Lord. We strongly suggest using this prayer form whether in individual or group study.

GROUP-STUDY FORMATS

1. Bible Study With *Lectio Divina*

About ninety minutes of group study
- ✠ Gathering and opening prayer (3–5 minutes)
- ✠ Scripture passage read aloud (5 minutes)
- ✠ Silently review the commentary and prepare to discuss it with the group (3–5 minutes)
- ✠ Discuss the Scripture passage along with the commentary and reflection (30 minutes)
- ✠ Scripture passage read aloud a second time, followed by quiet time for meditation and contemplation (5 minutes)
- ✠ Spend some time in prayer with the selected passage. Group participants will slowly read the Scripture passage a third time in silence, listening for the voice of God as they read (10–20 minutes)
- ✠ Shared reflection (10–15 minutes)
- ✠ Closing prayer (3–5 minutes)

To become acquainted with lectio divina, *see page 11.*

2. Bible Study

About one hour of group study
- ✠ Gathering and opening prayer (3–5 minutes)
- ✠ Scripture passage read aloud (5 minutes)
- ✠ Silently review the commentary and prepare to discuss it with the group (3–5 minutes)
- ✠ Discuss the Scripture passage along with the commentary and reflection (40 minutes)
- ✠ Closing prayer (3–5 minutes)

Notes to the Leader

- ✠ Bring a copy of the *New American Bible,* revised edition.
- ✠ Plan which sections will be covered each week of your Bible study.
- ✠ Read the material in advance of each session.
- ✠ Establish written ground rules. (Example: We won't keep you longer than ninety minutes; don't dominate the sharing by arguing or debating.)
- ✠ Meet in an appropriate and welcoming gathering space (church building, meeting room, house).
- ✠ Provide name tags and perhaps use a brief icebreaker for the first meeting; ask participants to introduce themselves.
- ✠ Mark the Scripture passage(s) that will be read during the session.
- ✠ Decide how you would like the Scripture to be read aloud (whether by one or multiple readers).
- ✠ Use a clock or watch.
- ✠ Provide extra Bibles (or copies of the Scripture passages) for participants who don't bring their Bible.
- ✠ Ask participants to read "Introduction: Letters to the Corinthians" (page 19) before the first session.
- ✠ Tell participants which passages to study and urge them to read the passages and commentaries before the meeting.
- ✠ If you opt to use the *lectio divina* format, familiarize yourself with this prayer form ahead of time.

Notes to Participants

- ✠ Bring a copy of the *New American Bible,* revised edition.
- ✠ Read "Introduction: Letters to the Corinthians" (page 19) before the first session.
- ✠ Read the Scripture passages and commentaries before each session.
- ✠ Be prepared to share and listen respectfully. (This is not a time to debate beliefs or argue.)

Opening Prayer

Leader: O God, come to my assistance,

Response: O Lord, make haste to help me.

Leader: Glory be to the Father, and to the Son, and to the Holy Spirit...

Response: ...as it was in the beginning, is now, and ever shall be, world without end. Amen.

Leader: Christ is the vine and we are the branches. As branches linked to Jesus, the vine, we are called to recognize that the Scriptures are always being fulfilled in our lives. It is the living Word of God living on in us. Come, Holy Spirit, fill the hearts of your faithful, and kindle in us the fire of your divine wisdom, knowledge, and love.

Response: Open our minds and hearts as we study your great love for us as shown in the Bible.

Reader: (Open your Bible to the assigned Scripture(s) and read in a paced, deliberate manner. Pause for one minute, listening for a word, phrase, or image that you may use in your *lectio divina* practice.)

Closing Prayer

Leader: Let us pray as Jesus taught us.

Response: Our Father...

Leader: Lord, inspire us with your Spirit as we study your Word in the Bible. Be with us this day and every day as we strive to know you and serve you and to love as you love. We believe that through your goodness and love, the Spirit of the Lord is truly upon us. Allow the words of the Bible, your Word, to capture us and inspire us to live as you live and to love as you love.

Response: Amen.

Leader: May the divine assistance remain with us always.

Response: In the name of the Father, and of the Son, and of the Holy Spirit. Amen.

Letters to the Corinthians

Read this overview before the first session.

Some years ago, a young girl wrote to a journalist expressing her sadness at discovering from her friends that Santa Claus did not really exist. The journalist wrote a classic reply to the young girl's letter in the newspaper, and it began with the famous words, "Yes, Virginia, there is a Santa Claus." He told her of all the wonders and dreams of life, and he explained that these were all signs of the presence of Santa Claus in the world.

Letters have been written throughout history to assist people who have suddenly come upon some unforeseen difficulties in their life. Before they died, some parents have written letters to their children so that the children could read the letters later in life and remember what hopes the parents had for them. Some of history's great writers have had their letters collected and printed so that later generations might learn from their wisdom. For many people, writing a letter is a way for them to express deep, personal thoughts to another person, something they may be unable to do face-to-face.

Paul is writing to the church of God he founded in Corinth. His letters to the Corinthians read like letters from a concerned parent who wishes to share wisdom—and a warning—with his or her children. Paul has received some disturbing news about the people he knows well and loves. The letters reflect his own suffering as well as his desire for the Corinthians to remain faithful to his teachings. Paul notes that he can sound more forceful when writing than when speaking in person, but he warns that he will not hesitate to speak forcefully in person if he must do so. Paul demonstrates the value and power of letter writing. In reading Paul's letters to the Corinthians, we gain an insight into his personality. He can be harsh if he must be, but he does not enjoy or delight in addressing the Corinthians in a harsh manner. Like a concerned parent, he worries about the manner in which they will receive his letters. He writes his letters not to berate them, but to correct them so that they may use their gifts well.

The letters to the Corinthians offer an interesting insight into one early church community as the members of the community attempt to live a life with this new message about Christ. The community has received an abundance of gifts and, surprisingly, these gifts have become a matter of division rather than unity. The gifts are new to the community, and Paul must address how to create orderly and correct use of these gifts. Even the celebration of the sacrament of baptism becomes a matter of division as members of one group claim superiority over others because of the apostle who baptized them.

Despite their many spiritual gifts, some in the community are still attempting to live a life in accord with Paul's teachings about Christ, while at the same time basing their judgments on earthly norms. In his letters to the Corinthians, Paul indicates that some are strong in the faith and realize that meat sacrificed to idols is not really offered to the gods because the gods do not exist. Others still coming into the faith must learn gradually that these false gods do not exist. Those with more mature faith must make sacrifices in order not to scandalize those who are just learning the faith.

The Author

The Acts of the Apostles narrates the story of Saul whose name became Paul in Greek and who was chosen by God to be an apostle to the Gentiles. Paul originally persecuted Christians but eventually converted to Christ and became a missionary to those whom he persecuted. Later, on a missionary journey with Barnabas, he was rejected along with Barnabas by the Jews in the synagogue at Antioch in Pisidia. Paul and Barnabas stated that it was necessary for them to preach first to the Jews, but since they were rejected, they turned to the Gentiles. They declared that the Lord chose them, saying, "I have made you a light to the Gentiles, that you may be an instrument of salvation to the ends of the earth" (13:47). This accounts for Paul's letters being written to Gentile audiences.

At the beginning of both letters to the Corinthians, Paul declares he is the author. By the end of the first century, Clement of Rome provided further evidence that Paul the Apostle is the author of these letters by making a reference to them. The Pauline authorship of these letters is also supported by the Moratorium fragments, which authenticate many early writings. The style, content, and manner of speaking in these letters also leave us with little doubt that Paul is their author.

The Acts of the Apostles (18:1–18) gives an account of Paul's activity among the Corinthians. Paul came to Corinth around the year 50 during his second missionary journey, and he settled there for approximately eighteen months. By his own admission, Paul began his ministry to the Corinthians with deep fear (1 Corinthians 2:3). At Corinth, Paul stayed for a period of time with a Jewish couple and preached each week in the synagogue, attempting to explain that Jesus was the Messiah, but the Jews in the synagogue opposed him. As a result, Paul shook out his garments, a common gesture in Paul's time used to show some form of rejection. He used the gesture to signal his rejection of his mission to the Jews and went to stay at the house of a Gentile.

The house in which Paul resided belonged to Titus Justus, the place where he began preaching to the Gentiles. We will read about Titus Justus in Paul's letters to the Corinthians. Furthermore, Paul converted a synagogue leader named Crispus and his household, along with many Corinthians. In 1 Corinthians (1:14), Paul speaks of Crispus as one of the few he himself baptized. The Lord appeared to Paul and encouraged him not to fear, but to go on preaching.

After eighteen months at Corinth, Paul had converted many Gentiles to faith in Jesus Christ. Sometime after he left the city, Paul received word of difficulties within the Corinthian church, and he wrote these letters in response to these difficulties.

Audience

The Romans destroyed the ancient city of Corinth about 146 BC. A century later, Julius Caesar ordered the city rebuilt. Because it had ports on two seas, Corinth became a natural center for trade between the East and the West. The city became a melting pot of all the trends and attitudes of the day, particularly the corruption involved in shipping and trading. Among those who lived in Corinth were Roman citizens, Jews, merchants from distant ports, and the native people of the area. In the ancient world, Corinth became identified with all the evils of the day, including temple prostitution. Pagan worship was rampant in the city. Paul preached about Christ in this corrupt city and converted many Gentiles to faith in Christ. The founding of a Christian community in such an atmosphere indicates the energy, courage, and faith of Paul. The faithfulness of the Corinthians to Paul shows that he instilled a strong faith in the hearts of the Corinthians who would now have to live their faith in this corrupt atmosphere.

Place and Date of Corinthians

Although Paul speaks in his First Letter to the Corinthians about his mission in Macedonia, the letter was most likely not written from that area. Macedonia encompassed a large territory located between the Greek peninsula and the Balkan highlands in southeastern Europe. Originally part of the Greek kingdom, it later became a Roman province and was part of the Roman Empire in Paul's era.

Paul spent some time at Ephesus, and most commentators believe he wrote his First Letter to the Corinthians from this city. Ephesus was an ancient Greek city, which, like Macedonia, later became part of the Roman Empire. It was a large city on the west coast of Asia Minor, near present-day Turkey. It is not easy to date the letter, because some time must be allowed for the community at Corinth to have developed to the point at which the letter would have been warranted. Because Paul mentions that Gallio was proconsul at the time of his visit to Corinth, we can date his missionary activity there somewhere after the year 50 (Acts 18:12–17). At the time, Gallio served as proconsul of the area for a single year. Some commentators date the letter as early as 53, but many others opt for the year 56 or 57.

Although commentators refer to the first letter as the "first" to the Corinthians, most commentators believe Paul wrote an earlier letter that has been lost. This one is the first of the letters of Paul to the Corinthians that history has been able to recover. Paul's Second Letter to the Corinthians appears to be a collection of several letters of Paul put together by an editor. Some commentators believe Paul himself gathered this small collection of letters into his Second Letter to the Corinthians.

Outline of 1 Corinthians

Condemnation of Disorders in the Corinthian Church (1—4)
Paul begins this letter with the usual greetings and thanksgivings before launching into the reason for the letter. He learned that factions exist among the Corinthians, and he challenges them to live the Christian message, looking toward the foolishness of the cross and their own lack of wisdom. True wisdom is not the wisdom of the world, but the wisdom given by the Spirit. The factions among the Corinthians show that they have not yet grasped the true meaning of the message. It is the message, not the messenger, that is the source of true wisdom.

Moral Disorders (5—11:1)
Paul lists the disorders found in the Corinthian community and instructs its members in correct behavior. A man having sexual relations with his stepmother should be cast out of the community for the sake of his own change of heart as well as for the sake of the community. Freedom in Christ does not lead to sexual license, because the body of the baptized is a temple of the Holy Spirit. Marriage and celibacy are important, and the believer should continue to live with the unbeliever as long as it does not lead to any problems for the believer. One should be willing to refrain from the eating of meat sacrificed to idols for the sake of the weak. To share at the table of idols, however, is to share in a conflict with the eucharistic celebration, which is the table of the Lord. The guiding principle is to do all for the glory of God, as Paul himself does in imitation of Christ.

Conduct at Worship and Spiritual Gifts (11:2—14:40)
Paul discusses the role of women in worship and states that all should gather at the Lord's Supper with loving concern. The gifts that come from the Spirit are given for the common good, the body of Christ. Rather than look for passing gifts, the Christian should seek the lasting gift of love. This gift will lead a person to seek the gifts that benefit and build up the community. Within the assembly, the use of these gifts should be reasonable and orderly.

The Resurrection (15:1–58)

For the members of the Corinthian community who do not believe in resurrection from the dead, Paul points out that Christ was raised first and that all others will share in a similar resurrection. Although they might deny resurrection by their words, their practice states otherwise; they accept the example of Paul and baptism for the sake of the dead. The body that is raised is a glorified body, unlike our natural body.

The Collection (16:1–24)

Paul concludes by instructing the people to set aside monetary gifts for the Christians of Jerusalem. He expresses his plans and sends greetings to the people of Corinth from himself and others with him.

Outline of 2 Corinthians

Opening Address (1:1–11)

Paul introduces himself as the sender of the letter and as an apostle. He offers thanksgiving for the reception the Corinthians have given to his letters and for their ability to endure what they must for the faith.

Crisis (1:12—7:16)

Paul explains that he intended to visit the Corinthians, but he was detained. He urges the community to forgive an offender and expresses his concern for his companion Titus who eventually joined him. He speaks of being a minister of the New Covenant and contrasts it with the Old Covenant. Recognizing the difficulties endured by the Corinthians, he stresses his afflictions and compares them to earthen vessels. He sees the new community through the eyes of Christ and states that he came in sincerity, not wishing to cause anyone to stumble. And he calls upon the Corinthians to live up to the holiness to which they are called. Finally, he rejoices when he receives news that the Corinthians have reconciled themselves to his message.

The Collection for Jerusalem (8:1—9:15)

Paul continues to urge the Corinthians to take up a collection for the Church in Jerusalem, and he commends them for their generosity. He sends Titus to care for the collection.

Paul's Defense of His Ministry (10:1—13:10)

Paul boasts of his sufferings, his labors, his visions, and his weakness. He does this not to boast of himself, but to build up the faith of the Corinthians.

Conclusion (13:11–13)

He ends with words of encouragement and blesses them, naming the Father, Son, and Holy Spirit (Trinitarian blessing).

> NOTE: When the letters are designated as 1 Corinthians and 2 Corinthians, the reader must realize that Paul is writing to the Corinthians who accepted faith in Jesus as the Christ, not a letter to everyone in the city of Corinth. Throughout this study, the term Corinthians is used to designate only those who were converted to Christ.

Condemnation of Disorders

1 CORINTHIANS 1–2

The message of the cross is foolishness to those who are perishing, but to us who are being saved it is the power of God (1:18).

Opening Prayer (SEE PAGE 18)

Context

Paul is writing to a community of Christians he established in Corinth. He greets the Corinthians and prays for God's blessings on them, thanking God that they at one time received God's message so well. After this friendly greeting, Paul launches into the reason for his letter, which was to correct the divisions he heard were occurring in the church in Corinth. Some people are bragging about belonging to Paul, while others are claiming to belong to Apollos or Cephas (Peter). Paul reminds them that they belong to Christ and calls them to accept the foolishness of the cross as a way of life. The wisdom of the cross does not stem from worldly knowledge, Paul instructs, but should be the only source of their boasting. Paul did not come to them with sublime words of wisdom, but with spirit and power. He was teaching them a spiritual message that cannot be understood by the natural person, but by the spiritual person. Christians, through faith, are gifted with the mind of Christ.

GROUP STUDY (1 CORINTHIANS 1—2)

Read aloud 1 Corinthians 1—2.

1:1–9 Greetings and thanksgiving

Paul begins with the usual format used in letters of his day. He immediately names himself as the sender, and the church of God at Corinth as the one to whom the letter is being sent. He also refers to himself as an apostle of Jesus Christ, a title that identifies his ministry as one of authority. Paul does not declare himself an apostle in the sense used for the Twelve who are witnesses to the public life of Jesus but as an apostle who is chosen in a unique manner for the mission of proclaiming the message of Jesus Christ. He says he is called to be an apostle of Jesus Christ "by the will of God" (1:1). In his letters, Paul often identifies himself as an apostle, since some Christians remember him as a persecutor of the followers of Christ. Others limited their view of apostles to the Twelve.

Paul names Sosthenes as his companion and as one who joins with him in sending greetings to the Corinthians. In the Acts of the Apostles, a man named Sosthenes is a synagogue leader in Corinth, who is dragged before a proconsul by the Jews and is beaten in the presence of the proconsul. When Paul was in Corinth, the Jewish leaders of the area brought Paul before the tribunal and accused him of stirring up the people by inducing them to worship contrary to the law. Although the author does not tell us whether his teachings are contrary to Roman law or the Mosaic Law, the reaction of Gallio, the proconsul, shows that he judged it to be a teaching contrary to Jewish law and declares that their problem is one of doctrine for them to solve. He adds that if it were a matter of some crime or malicious action, he would listen to their complaint.

Because the Jewish leaders of the area were not able to vent their wrath against Paul, they chose to persecute Sosthenes in his place. We know little about Sosthenes and do not even know why they chose him as a victim for the beating (see Acts 18:12–17). Since the beating took place in Corinth, the companion mentioned in the First Letter to the Corinthians may have been this same Sosthenes, but this is inconclusive, since the name was a common one. Sosthenes may have played some part in forming this letter, but it seems to have been a very minor part.

Paul apparently has an underlying message for the Corinthians in the manner in which he addresses them—as "the church of God that is in Corinth." His purpose was likely intended to remind the people at Corinth that they do not exist alone but that they belong to a larger Church of God and that they must strive for unity with this larger Church. This unity of the churches is important to Paul, because it reflects the Hebrew idea of the unity of the people of God. As the new people of God, Christians must recognize their unity with one another. Although the Corinthians received many gifts from the Lord, they should not view themselves as superior to the other churches established by Paul.

Paul also addresses the Corinthians as those called to be a holy people, sanctified in Jesus Christ. This manner of address comes from Paul's understanding of the sanctification and change that occurs at baptism. In their baptism, the Corinthians now belong to a holy people, just as the Israelites of the Old Testament were called to be a holy people of God.

As a further sign of the unity that exists among all the churches, Paul broadens the greetings in the introduction to include all peoples of all churches, wherever they may be. He shows his concern for the universal Church, and not just the church of God at Corinth. Finally, he wishes his audience the customary grace and peace that place them in harmony with God the Father and Christ.

Paul follows the ordinary custom found in letters of the day by offering thanks for gifts received. He thanks God for the gift of God's blessing and favor that the Corinthians received through Jesus Christ. Since he witnessed these gifts when he was living among them, Paul is able to declare that they have been blessed with many gifts of speech and knowledge that come through Jesus. He affirms that they lack none of the gifts given by God as they await the revealing of our Lord Jesus Christ. The revealing of our Lord Jesus Christ will occur at the Second Coming of Christ, a constant theme in the letters of Paul. These gifts will enable them to be firm in faith until the end time. The Corinthians can be assured that until that time, God, who is faithful, will continue to share these gifts with all those called to unity with the Son, whom he identifies as our Lord Jesus Christ.

Although Paul thanks God for the gifts given to the Corinthians, he does not thank God for the gifts of faith, hope, and love that are found in this part of some of his other letters. Because Paul is writing this letter in response to some of the problems that have arisen in Corinth, he most likely omitted this part of the thanksgiving to challenge his audience to practice these virtues when using the gifts they received through Christ. He reminds the Corinthians that God, who called them into union with Jesus, will always be faithful to that call. The implication is that the Corinthians are the ones who have not been faithful. In Paul's view, faith, hope, and love, which should be a result of the gifts they received, are lacking in the lives of the Corinthians.

1:10–17 Divisions in the church

Some servants from the household of Chloe have informed Paul about a division that exists among the members of the church at Corinth. This is the only mention of Chloe and her household in the Scriptures. Since Paul can name Chloe without giving any further details to his Corinthian audience, we can deduce that she was well known to the members of the Corinthian church. Paul trusts the message brought by the members of her household and responds to it in this letter.

He implores his audience, whose members have become one in Christ through baptism, to dispel all divisions and to come to a common accord and unity as is fitting for all those baptized into the one Christ. The basis of the problem seems to be the boasting of some members of the community concerning the one who taught and baptized them. The boasting is not against the idea of baptism itself or the ritual for baptizing. Some members of the community say they belong to Paul, others to a famous preacher in Corinth named Apollos (see Acts 18:24–28), others to Cephas, and finally others to Christ. When Paul refers to Peter, he often uses the name Cephas. As far as we know, Cephas never visited Corinth, but his fame must have spread to this city as it did throughout the Christian world. There may have been some who were baptized elsewhere by Peter and later migrated to Corinth.

Paul asks his audience with a tone of sarcasm whether they think that Christ has been divided into parts. The obvious answer, of course, is no.

Paul ignores the other factions and reproaches those who claim they belong to Paul. He asks if he were the one crucified for them, and again the answer is no. Paul is grateful that he has performed only a few baptisms at Corinth, not because it was beneath his dignity, but because of the problems now arising from divisions among the Christians of the area. Those in the community who claim to belong to certain factions within the church of God at Corinth cannot say they belong to Paul because he baptized them. Paul admits that he baptized the household of a man named Stephanas, but he is not sure whether he has baptized anyone else. His inability to remember whether he baptized anyone else may arise from the many people he converted to Christ. His stay at Corinth was one of turmoil and confusion. Paul views his ministry as one of preaching, leaving the celebration of baptism to others.

Furthermore, Paul admits his preaching may not be as eloquent as that of others, and he is grateful he does not have this ability. Apollos, on the other hand, was an eloquent preacher who was well respected and accepted by the people. Paul is grateful that the message of the cross is the true wisdom behind his preaching; the power of the cross should speak for itself. Although today we accept Jesus' crucifixion and death on the cross with ease, Paul had the difficulty of convincing people that Jesus, who died a criminal's death, was really the Christ. Because Paul believes that power is revealed in weakness, he trusts that the message of the cross is powerful in itself. He will expound on the message of the cross of Jesus Christ.

1:18—2:5 Wisdom of the cross

Paul preaches the message of the cross as foolishness to those who do not believe and are facing spiritual destruction but as a sign of God's power for those who believe and are sharing in salvation. He quotes from Isaiah, showing that God has already spoken of confounding the wise and clever people of the world. In light of the foolishness of the cross that brings salvation, the wise and clever become the ones who are truly foolish (Isaiah 29:14).

During Jesus' public life, his opponents demanded some sign that he was the Messiah (Matthew 16:1–4). The Jewish people believed there would be unmistakable signs that would clearly point out the Messiah. Paul knows this belief in signs is at the root of Jewish thought, and he proclaims that the Jews want signs while the Greeks, the lovers of knowledge, seek wisdom. Both are frustrated by the preaching of the cross of Jesus Christ. The Jews see the one who is crucified as a "stumbling block" because, in Jewish thought, he is cursed. Many of the people of Judea believed crucifixion was not only a humiliating end to life but a sign of God's disfavor. The Greeks conceive preaching about a crucified Jesus as contrary to wisdom and perfectly absurd. In their eyes, only criminals were crucified.

Paul declares that for those who believe in Christ, whether Jew or Greek, Jesus' death on the cross is a sign of God's power and wisdom. Paul realizes that Jesus has conquered death through his resurrection. The foolishness of God is much wiser than human wisdom, and the weakness of God is stronger than any human strength. Paul asks the Corinthians, who are called to share in this foolishness of Christ, to take a good look at themselves. According to the standards of the world, few of these people were considered wise, influential, or well born. Just as God chose the cross to confound the wise and the strong, so now God chooses the foolish and weak to shame them. In doing so, God enables all people to realize that no one has a right to boast, since Jesus Christ himself has become the real source of their boasting. For the believer, Christ is the wisdom, the righteousness, the sanctification, and the redemption of all. Paul adapts a quotation from the prophet Jeremiah (9:23) that states that all boasting, if necessary at all, must be done in the Lord. Jeremiah was applying these words to God, the Lord of all, while Paul applies them to Jesus Christ.

As we continue to read this letter to the Corinthians, we discover the true powerlessness of Paul in relationship to people like Apollos. He apparently has little to offer in the way of personal appearance and speech, but he finds his power in the message of the gospel. He tells his audience that he did not come with the worldly gifts of eloquence or wisdom. He had no intention of seeking self-approval; he simply wanted to speak about the crucified Jesus Christ.

When Paul preaches about Jesus crucified, he always has in mind the resurrection of Jesus, as we discover in a later section of this letter (15:1–11). Because of the resurrection, the message of the cross is no longer a message of foolishness or absurdity. Paul emphasizes the message of the cross in this letter to the Corinthians because he seems to believe that the Corinthian community has ignored this aspect of it.

Paul does not face his audience with a brazen confidence but, instead, tells the Corinthians that he first came among them with his human weakness, trembling in fear. This may have arisen out of fear that the Corinthians would not receive him. Paul came to Corinth from Athens, and his experience in that city was one of rejection and persecution (Acts 17:16–34). He hoped he would fare better in Corinth, but he did not know what lay in store for him.

Paul recognized that the Spirit had to make up for those gifts that were lacking in his human appearance. With no power of eloquence or wisdom, he depended entirely on the power of the Spirit working through him. Now, as he writes to the Corinthians, he can declare that their faith rests, not on his gifts, but entirely on the power of God.

2:6–16 True wisdom

Paul declares that he is sharing wisdom with his readers, but it is a wisdom not easily grasped by those who are not spiritually mature. The people and the rulers of the age whose hearts look toward the wisdom of this world are really seeking an empty, destructive wisdom. Paul warns against this worldly wisdom because he sees it as the root of the divisions he challenges in this letter.

The wisdom Paul offers his readers comes from the unsearchable depths of God. Paul speaks of a wisdom of God, a hidden mystery that God pre-determined from the beginning for the glory of believers. The decision to put Jesus to death proved that the rulers of the age lacked all knowledge of this wisdom. If they'd had this wisdom, they would have recognized that Jesus would conquer the power of evil in the world through his crucifixion and resurrection. If they wished to protect their evil powers, they would not have allowed Jesus to overcome them through his death and resurrection. Quoting from Isaiah (64:3), Paul reminds readers that God had already spoken of this spiritual wisdom. Isaiah writes that the eyes, ears, and minds of humans have not understood the gift prepared for those who love God.

This wisdom of God comes to us through a revelation of the Spirit.

Because human beings cannot fully comprehend the depths of God, Paul looks in another direction for this power to understand God's ways. Conscious of God's fullness, the Spirit reveals the wisdom of God to believers. Just as the spirit of the human person is able to understand the depths of that person, so the Spirit of God alone is able to understand the depths of God, therein revealing God to us. Because worldly wisdom cannot help us understand this revelation of God, we need the Spirit of the Lord, which has been given to us to understand God's wisdom.

The message of the cross is not a message for the worldly wise, who are incapable of understanding it. The true message of the cross must be taught by the Spirit, and it is the Spirit working in us that helps us understand Christ's message. For those who live only according to natural wisdom, the message of the Spirit (the cross) is foolish and absurd. Only by looking at this message in its full spiritual sense can a person truly understand it.

Paul reminds the Corinthians that one living according to natural wisdom will not truly understand the wisdom of the spiritual person. The person who lives by the Spirit of God, however, has the insight to understand the workings of God. Drawing on some Old Testament texts and adapting them to fit his message, Paul asks who can claim to understand the mind of God to the point of believing that they could counsel God. The answer, of course, is no one. Through the gift of the Spirit, we have the mind of Christ, which enables us to understand God's spiritual mysteries.

Review Questions

1. How does the message to "the church of God that is in Corinth" apply to our parish family today?

2. Can the divisions found in the church of Corinth be seen in our parish and universal Church communities today? What might the church of Corinth teach us about our arguments over matters of faith?

3. Is a rosary blessed by the pope more holy than a rosary blessed by the pastor of a parish? Why or why not? Explain.

4. Contemplate the "foolishness of the cross" as described by Paul. How might we apply it to our self-understanding today? Our prayer life?

5. Identify and name some examples of Paul's idea of true wisdom.

Closing Prayer (SEE PAGE 18)

Pray the closing prayer at this time or after *lectio divina*.

Lectio Divina (SEE PAGE 11)

Relax your body and maintain a posture of prayer (back straight, eyes shut, feet flat on the floor). This exercise can take as long as you want, but in the context of this Bible study, 10 to 20 minutes should be sufficient.

The meditations that follow are provided only to help group participants use this prayer form, but note that *lectio* is intended to bring one to a place of prayerful contemplation where the Word of God speaks to the hearer from his or her heart. (See page 11 for further instruction.)

Greetings and thanksgiving (1:1–9)

Paul tells the Corinthians that they have received the call to be holy, and he adds that "all those everywhere who call upon the name of our Lord Jesus Christ" are called to be holy. Whenever an individual asked a saintly nun to pray for him or her, she would answer that she would pray some special prayers for that person. The person would leave, believing the nun would offer a prayer for him or her sometime during the day. The nun did pray for the person, but she would also pick up the phone after the individual left and call an elderly woman friend who lived in the parish. The nun knew this woman was a humble woman who prayed often and was close to God. She believed her own prayers were strong, but she believed the prayers of this saintly woman were far more powerful.

Many people view clergy and religious as the ones called to be holier than others in the Church. The Church teaches, however, that clergy and religious have a call to live holy lives, but so does everyone else. All the baptized receive the call to be a holy people. Since a person's saintliness is not easily seen, we cannot determine who is holier than others. We are all called to be as saintly as we can be and leave the rest up to God. Paul's immediate challenge for the Corinthians and all the baptized is to live holy and saintly lives. We, too, are included in Paul's universal call to holiness.

✠ *What can I learn from this passage?*

Divisions in the Church (1:10–17)

Paul is confronted with a foolish reason for division where the members of one group wish to prove they are better than others because of who baptized them. As Christians, we may have differences, but these differences should never become a reason for turning against others in the assembly.

There is a humorous story adapted to life in the Church. A man asks his pastor if standing throughout the eucharistic celebration is considered tradition. The pastor answers, "No." The man then asks the pastor whether kneeling is considered tradition. The pastor answers, "No." The man says, "In my parish, some people argue over whether standing or kneeling is tradition. At times, these arguments can become heated with a lot of harsh words and rage." The pastor answers, "Now, that's tradition."

As holy as we strive to be, we still find a large number of differing opinions in the Church regarding many matters, and in some cases, the arguments may become heated. Differences exist, but they should not be a cause of division. All the baptized are called to unity, harmony, holiness, and peace. Paul is saddened by the divisions existing in the church of God at Corinth.

✠ *What can I learn from this passage?*

Wisdom of the cross (1:18—2:5)

We should never seek suffering for its own sake, and when we are in pain, we should seek to alleviate the pain using moral means. Paul taught that Jesus provided a new understanding of the prayerfulness involved in suffering and pain. Jesus' suffering brought salvation to the world, and the suffering we endure in life can bring blessings upon ourselves and others when we place our suffering in union with that of Jesus.

A man who was near death and suffering terribly wondered why God did not take him from his painful and apparently useless life. He believed, however, that since he was still alive, God must have more for him to do. The suffering man was bedridden and riddled with unbearable pain, but he believed his suffering was a powerful form of prayer. People without faith would look at this man and protest that he was indeed a fool. There are some who would seek escape from such pain, even to the point of seeking assisted suicide. Jesus taught us that suffering and pain can have merit.

To the world, such weakness and pain are foolishness, but to Paul, the foolishness of such a cross can bring salvation and suffering, depending on what people do with their suffering. Jesus remained true to his mission when he could have had a legion of angels free him from the cross. Paul tells us, "For the foolishness of God is wiser than human wisdom, and the weakness of God is stronger than human strength."

What can I learn from this passage?

True wisdom (2:6–16)

Paul speaks of living with trust in the Spirit. The natural person lives only by what he or she sees, while the spiritual person is able to look beyond the events of life to see the hand of God in creation. Those living in the Spirit can recognize the continual presence of God in their lives. This is the wisdom of those who believe.

A man declared that each morning when he awoke, he would use the same words that he heard from waiters in a restaurant. He would say, "Good morning, Jesus. My name is Bill, and I'll be your servant today." In this way, he was offering his day to God as a prayer. He believed that whatever happened in his day was a prayer and that God was his constant companion in whatever work God called him to perform.

Jesus told his disciples that they would receive the Spirit of truth "which the world cannot accept, because it neither sees nor knows it"(John 14:17). As Christians, we witness the presence of God in our joys, our works, our sufferings, our successes, and our failures. Living as a Christian means we must live at a deeper level than that which is seen with our eyes and with our touch. It is a realization that there is more to life than the world we physically experience. For that reason, we can offer our day to God as a living prayer. Paul tells us that "we speak of God's wisdom, mysterious, hidden."

What can I learn from this passage?

INDIVIDUAL STUDY

This lesson does not have an individual-study component.

Temples of the Holy Spirit

1 CORINTHIANS 3—7

Do you not know that your body is a temple of the holy Spirit within you, whom you have from God, and that you are not your own. For you have been purchased at a price. Therefore, glorify God in your body (6:19–20).

Opening Prayer (SEE PAGE 18)

Context

Part 1: 1 Corinthians 3—4 Paul views the Corinthians as spiritual children who had to be fed spiritual milk because they were still greatly influenced by the world. The proof is in their attitude, which led to their bragging about belonging to Paul or Apollos or Cephas. Ministers for Christ work together, with one planting and another harvesting, or one laying the foundation and another building. All must fulfill their task well. They must act as trustworthy stewards. Paul offers his life and that of Apollos as a pattern. Paul warns them that they should beware of boasting and declares that he is weak, while sarcastically stating that they are strong. Likewise, he warns them that he will come and face those inflated with pride. They can choose whether he should come to berate them or treat them gently and with love.

Part 2: 1 Corinthians 5—7 In these passages, Paul addresses moral disorders within Corinth. He bemoans those who are practicing incest and urges the people not to mingle with those who are sinful. Paul laments over those within the Christian community who are suing one another in pagan courts and warns against sexual immorality, reminding the Corinthians that their bodies are temples of the Holy Spirit. He talks about the relationship between a husband and wife and urges celibacy for the unmarried and widowed. The circumcised are to remain circumcised and the slaves are to remain slaves, but slaves should see themselves as free in the Lord. He speaks of practical problems of living as a virgin or a married person and the spiritual advantages and difficulties of each.

PART 1: GROUP STUDY (1 CORINTHIANS 3—4)

Read aloud 1 Corinthians 3—4.

3:1–15 The role of God's ministers

In the previous passage, Paul made a distinction between those who were spiritually mature and those who lived with the wisdom of the world. He now tells his listeners that they were not spiritually mature but more like "fleshly people," that is, worldly people. In their desire to learn about Jesus, they had learned as though they were spiritual infants in Christ. Paul tells them he gave them milk, that is, he presented his message in such a way that they could begin to grasp it. Since, like infants, they could not accept solid food, he kept his message simple. Even now, Paul tells them, they are still spiritual infants, not ready for solid food. The proof of their adherence to their natural selves can be seen in the divisions in the community, signs that they are people who judge according to worldly standards. The mere fact that they label themselves as followers of Paul or followers of Apollos is proof that they are living according to human norms.

Paul uses the image of farming to teach that each minister of the gospel has a particular function and that all work together for the sake of the harvest. He declares that his role and that of Apollos are ministries given to them by God. As the founder of the church at Corinth, Paul was the one who planted the seed, and Apollos, who followed after Paul, was the one who watered the ground. God, however, is the one who performs the greater task—giving the church its growth. The planter and the waterer work for the sake of the same harvest, and they will receive their wages in accordance with their labors. Paul continues to exhort his readers that he and Apollos are coworkers with God, while the Corinthians are the field and the building. After using the image of farming for the Corinthians, the sudden use of the image of the Corinthians as a "building" may surprise the reader, since it has nothing to do with planting and growing. But the image is used to link this passage with the one that follows.

Paul continues to see himself as the founder of the community, the one who laid the foundation of the building of the church at Corinth. Another builds upon the foundation. The builder, however, must build correctly or the building will crumble. The foundation is Christ, and the builder has the duty to use sturdy materials for the building. The durability of the structure, or the lack of durability, will eventually identify the type of ministry performed by the builder. Paul is saying that the firm faith of the Corinthians depends not only on him, but on others who come after him to teach the Corinthians. All ministries work together for a successful outcome.

Paul turns his attention to the Day of Judgment, which he simply calls "the Day." On the Day of Judgment, the role of the worker will be tested. If the structure continues to withstand the fire of this day, the worker will receive a reward. For Paul, the reward seems to refer to the number of those who stand firm in the faith. If the structure does not withstand this final judgment, the ministers may be saved despite their poor ministry, but they will not receive the reward of seeing those to whom they ministered being firm in their faith. In writing these words, Paul may be giving a warning to a certain minister within the Corinthian community whom he does not name but whom he believes is not building the faith of the people in a proper manner.

3:16–23 Temples of God

Paul now uses the image of a spiritual temple for the first time in this letter. The concept of a temple is sacred to both Jews and Greeks alike, and Paul calls the church of Corinth a temple of God. The temple was the dwelling place of God. The temple in which the Spirit dwells among the Corinthians is not a temple built of stone, but a temple composed of members of the Corinthian church. Paul warns those who would destroy this temple that in so doing, they will be destroyed by God. He is speaking to those who preach a message contrary to the message of the gospel. To lead members of the Corinthian church away from the gospel message is to destroy the temple of the Spirit. Because of this presence of the Spirit, the temple can be called a "holy" temple.

Paul had to contend with a group who apparently considered themselves intellectuals with true wisdom. Paul warns them that they are deceiving themselves, and so invites them to become fools for the sake of true wisdom. Those who think of themselves as wise in the ways of the world are actually the ones God sees as foolish. Paul quotes from Job (5:13), who speaks of the wise as catching themselves in their own clever traps, and he quotes from Psalms (94:11), showing that God is always aware of the emptiness of worldly wisdom.

Paul urges these supposed "intellectuals" to cease their boasting, since they have received everything from Christ. They do not belong to anyone or anything; instead they belong to Christ, who is God.

4:1–21 Following the example of Paul

Paul tells his readers that he and other preachers of the gospel should be regarded as servants and stewards of God's gifts and nothing more. They administer the mysteries of God, a reference to the spiritual message and gifts that come from Jesus. A major virtue for stewards is to be trustworthy servants, because the master depends on them to distribute the gifts in the master's name.

Paul believes he has served well as an administrator of God's gifts, and he does not look to the Corinthians for their judgment. Although he finds nothing to blame in himself, Paul realizes it is not his role to pass judgment on himself. The master, whom he or she represents, must do the judging. In this case, it is the Lord who will judge Paul. Because he expects this judgment at the time when the Lord returns, Paul warns the Corinthians not to waste their time judging him. At the time of the Second Coming, nothing will be hidden from God, and all will be revealed.

Paul uses himself and Apollos as examples, since the Christians of

Corinth have boasted of belonging to one or the other. Just as Paul or Apollos have avoided acting as though one were better than the other, so the Corinthians should not feel that some are better than others because they can boast of belonging to Paul or Apollos. He reminds his readers that neither he nor Apollos taught them to judge in this manner.

As he continues his exhortation, Paul appeals to the Corinthians to name those gifts they have merited on their own and have not received. Paul constantly teaches that no one merits the gifts that come to us from Christ. Because this is so, no one has a right to boast about those things that are strictly gifts given through Christ. Paul mocks the attitude of his readers that leads them to boast about their gifts as though they have reached the point of satisfaction, a wealth of knowledge, and a kingly state without help from Paul or Apollos. They are acting as though they reign with God without any help from those who preached the gospel. Paul sarcastically wishes that they were truly sharing in this reign so that he and Apollos could learn from them how to become kings like them.

During Paul's time, a conqueror would march in triumph at the head of the parade with his army immediately behind him. At the rear would march the prisoners and slaves from the lands he'd conquered, many of whom would be thrown to the wild animals in the arena. Paul sarcastically tells the Corinthians that they are like the conquerors at the head of the parade, while he and the other disciples are like the prisoners at the end of the parade who march to the slaughter. Like the people destined for the arena, Paul and Apollos accept the position of being the fools for Christ, weak and unworthy of respect, while the Corinthians appear to be wise in Christ and honored. Despite their foolishness for Christ, they are the truly wise ones who are willing to go hungry, thirsty, poorly clothed, mistreated, and homeless. They bless when insulted and speak kindly when slandered. According to worldly standards, they are the outcasts, the rubbish, and fools.

Paul changes his tone to that of a father who has brought the Corinthians to the faith in the first place. They have many guides, but only one father, namely, Paul. He writes to urge them to change their ways and to imitate him who first brought the gospel to them. Paul's concern and love for them are so great that he is willing to send Timothy to them, despite his great desire of having Timothy as a companion on his missionary journey. Timothy was apparently well known to the people of Corinth.

Finally, Paul challenges those who have made themselves important in his absence, and he promises to come to Corinth (if God is willing) to deal with these people. He will not judge them according to their words but according to their deeds, which Paul sees as a true sign of the reign of God among them. The Corinthians, like children, will determine whether Paul will come with a rod or with gentleness.

Review Questions

1. How can we apply Paul's message about planting and harvesting? In what way might God generate growth in our daily lives?

2. How does the knowledge that we are a temple of God, the dwelling place of the Holy Spirit, affect our manner of life?

3. Paul's teaches us through the Corinthians that we are servants and stewards of God's mysteries. How might we apply this understanding to our daily lives?

4. What is a fool for Christ according to Paul? Explain. Share how you might be challenged to be foolish for the sake of the reign of God.

5. What does Paul mean when he says he wants his readers to imitate him?

Closing Prayer (SEE PAGE 18)

Pray the closing prayer now or after *lectio divina*.

Lectio Divina (SEE PAGE 11)

Relax your body and maintain a posture of prayer (back straight, eyes shut, feet flat on the floor). This exercise can take as long as you want, but in the context of this Bible study, 10 to 20 minutes should be sufficient.

The meditations that follow are provided only to help group participants use this prayer form, but note that *lectio* is intended to bring one to a place of prayerful contemplation where the Word of God speaks to the hearer from his or her heart. (See page 11 for further instruction.)

The role of God's ministers (3:1–15)

Jesus spoke of the reign of God as likened to a seed that is sown and grows little by little, producing first the blade, then the ear, then the full grain of the ear (Mark 4:26–29). Paul realizes that our role in life is to plant seeds, nourish the seeds as needed, and finally bring in a harvest; but Paul also notes that the harvester is not always the planter.

A man once wrote about becoming a Christian because of his admiration of a fellow Christian prisoner while they were both in a concentration camp. The Christian prisoner, ignoring his own hunger, offered his food to others because they were hungry and in need of nourishment. Years later the man, who was fed and survived his ordeal, approached his pastor and asked to become Catholic.

Throughout our lives we are called to plant seeds, not transplant trees. In other words, our small actions are important in God's creation. No one can really boast that he or she is better than others, since God is the one who makes our mission fruitful. One plants, one harvests, and God gives the growth. The Christian man in the concentration camp planted the seed; the grace of God gave the seed growth, and the pastor reaped the harvest. That is the way God's creation works.

✠ *What can I learn from this passage?*

Temples of God (3:16–23)

The message of Paul elaborates on this simple acceptance of God's reign in our lives. We are temples of God, which means that the Spirit of God dwells in us. A Jesuit named Isaac Jogues was one of the first missionaries to come to the American continent. Seeking to bring the message of Christ to the natives of the area, he was captured and tortured horribly. A little more than a year later, he managed to escape and return to France. After recuperating and working in France, he asked to return to America, where he renewed his missionary ministry, despite its dangers. He was again captured, tortured, and finally killed.

To many people without faith, Saint Isaac Jogues was a fool. He suffered and died because he believed in something he could not see with his eyes. Isaac Jogues, however, believed he was an instrument of the Holy Spirit, a temple of God's presence, and his life meant less to him than the need to share Christ's message with others. The Apostle Paul would understand the motive of love of God driving Isaac Jogues. He warns that "the wisdom of this world is foolishness in the eyes of God."

Paul invites us to become foolish enough to realize that reality is often what we do not see and cannot measure. As Christians, we believe that we are temples of the Holy Spirit, with the Spirit of God dwelling in us and guiding us. This can sound like foolishness to the unbeliever, but it is reality to those who accept this truth with the faith of a small child.

✠ *What can I learn from this passage?*

Following the example of Paul (4:1–21)

Paul offers himself and Apollos as models for the people of Corinth. Just as they are willing to be fools for Christ, so the Corinthians should be willing to be fools for Christ by serving others.

A man named Tom took care of his wife when she became ill and was near death. After she died, he visited the elderly people in the neighborhood and offered to do their grocery shopping for them. Since he could not drive because of his age, he would purchase the groceries for a homebound person, put the groceries in his red wagon, and pull the wagon to the person's home. When he died, a number of people wanted to say something about him at his wake. Each one seemed to have the same theme: "Tom was a saint, a true servant of the people."

In John's Gospel, Jesus takes the role of a servant and washes the feet of his disciples, saying, "If I, therefore, the master and teacher, have washed your feet, you ought to wash one another's feet. I have given you a model to follow, so that as I have done for you, you should also do" (13:14–15). He invites us to follow his example, knowing that what really matters in life is serving Christ and others in the name of Christ. According to Paul, all gifts are given for the common good, not for the boasting of the one who receives the gift.

✠ *What can I learn from this passage?*

PART 2: INDIVIDUAL STUDY (1 CORINTHIANS 5—7)

Day 1: A Case of Incest (5:1–13)

Paul scolds the community for their acceptance of immorality in their midst. Besides the news of factions in Corinth, Paul declares that he also received news, perhaps from the household of Chloe, that the Corinthians are allowing a member of the community, who is committing incest by living with his stepmother, to live among them. He declares that even pagans condemn this sin. Jewish and Roman law both condemned marriage between a man and his stepmother. Paul views the acceptance of such a situation on the part of the Corinthians as a sign that they have abandoned the message he preached to them.

He continues by noting that the church community has the authority to excommunicate such a person, but the Corinthians have not done so. Rather than accepting this sin, the Corinthians should express great sorrow over it and expel the sinner from their community. Although he is not present in Corinth, Paul excommunicates that person in his letter, basing his right on the authority of Christ. As long as a person belongs to the Church, the Church must protect the person from destruction by Satan. Paul urges the community to turn this man over to Satan, not for the sake of condemning him, but for the sake of saving him. Perhaps in receiving this excommunication, he will experience a need to avoid sin and be able to save his spirit on Judgment Day.

Lectio Divina

Spend 8 to 10 minutes in silent contemplation of the following passage:

> When the scribes and the Pharisees accused Jesus of eating and drinking with sinners, Jesus responded, "I did not come to call the righteous but sinners" (Mark 2:17). Paul is astonished that someone would commit a sin of incest, which even pagans knew was not right, but Paul still sought that person's good. He wanted the person cut off from the community so that he would not contaminate them, but he also wanted a punishment that would lead to his salvation.

A woman who was very exacting with her religious practices lost her mother, father, and sixteen-year-old brother in a tragic car accident. She became bitter, blaming God for what happened. When she was participating in the eucharistic liturgy on the following Sunday, she suddenly felt she did not belong. The woman eventually turned completely against God, became wildly promiscuous, and drank alcohol until she could hardly stand. A year later, she awoke one Sunday morning beside a man she did not know and suddenly realized how aimless and unfulfilled her life had become. The night before, she had drunk heavily and could not remember how she came to sleep with this stranger. After showering and getting rid of the man, she ran to the noon liturgy being celebrated nearby and wept throughout the liturgy. She met with the pastor after worship, confessed her sins, and received absolution. She came back to God, humbled, repentant, and grateful for God's love in her life. She was a sinner who had returned.

Jesus' concern for sinners can prompt us to realize that instead of rejecting the sinner, we should pray for him or her and work for the person's salvation. In the Gospel of Luke, we read that the people of a Samaritan town did not welcome Jesus and his disciples because they were on a journey to Jerusalem. James and John ask Jesus if he wants them to call down fire from heaven to consume them. But Jesus rebukes them for such a thought (9:51–56). Jesus did not come to destroy sinners, but to call them to repentance. We never know the journey toward faith taken by those who are sinful.

✠ *What can I learn from this passage?*

Day 2: Our Bodies as Temples of the Holy Spirit (6:1–20)

Paul reproaches the Corinthian Christians for the practice of bringing one another before the pagan courts of Corinth rather than before the leaders within their own community. When Paul refers to these pagan courts as wicked and unjust, he is speaking of their lack of faith in the message of Jesus rather than any lack of honesty within the courts. Although dishonesty may have existed, it is not Paul's intention to condemn these courts. His rebuke is for the Christians in the community who make use of them.

Jewish tradition taught that those who follow the ways of God will judge the world. Paul applies this idea to the Christians who are now living in an age that he believes is the last age. He reminds them that they will be called upon to judge the whole world, and if this is so, they should be able to judge correctly the small matters of daily life. The judgment made by Jesus' followers will be so universal that Paul even includes in it the judgment of angels. The sin of the Corinthians is a sin of pride, yet their actions show that they have no confidence in themselves. Paul hopes to shame the Corinthians because of their attitude of choosing pagan judges to judge them. They do not have confidence enough to choose anyone in the community as a judge.

Paul goes a step further, telling the Corinthians that they should not have any reason for dragging one another into court in the first place. The mere fact that they follow the pagan practices of bringing lawsuits against one another shows they have already given way to the flesh. In Matthew's Gospel, we read that Jesus tells his followers to accept all injustice for the sake of the kingdom of God. Paul asks why they do not put up with injustice or with being cheated instead of inflicting cheating and injustice on one another. Those who are unjust will not inherit the kingdom of God. Paul knew from listening to the preaching about Jesus that Jesus warned the scribes and Pharisees that they would not enter the kingdom of God since they closed entry into God's kingdom to others (Matthew 23:13). Paul lists those who will not inherit the kingdom of God, including those guilty of sexual sins, idolatry, thievery, greed, drunkenness, or slander. He reminds his readers that at one time they were guilty of these sins, but now they have been washed, that is, baptized and justified in the name of Jesus Christ and the Spirit of God.

In speaking about the need to follow the practices of the Mosaic Law, Paul tells his listeners that they were no longer slaves to the law, but free from the law. Some of the Corinthians misinterpreted this freedom to mean freedom to commit whatever actions they wished, including those considered sinful. Some even went so far as to separate the body and human activities from the spirit of a person. They lived as if the body belonged to nature and would have no effect on the final outcome, so one could do whatever he or she wished with the body.

For Paul, however, the body refers to the whole person, and he reminds his readers that, through baptism, the body belongs to Christ. Just as God raised Jesus from the dead, so God will raise all people. Paul uses the Old Testament image of marriage that speaks of the two becoming one flesh (Genesis 2:24). The body joined to Christ is one with Christ, but the body joined to a prostitute becomes one with the prostitute. Just as a married person belongs to the spouse, so the Christian belongs to Christ. Paul tells his readers that they have been "purchased at a price," a reference to the death and resurrection of Jesus.

Lectio Divina

Spend 8 to 10 minutes in silent contemplation of the following passage:

In Luke's Gospel, Jesus enters a synagogue on the Sabbath and reads words from the prophet Isaiah that apply to him and to all who are baptized into Christ. He reads, "The Spirit of the Lord is upon me…"(4:18). Paul's words reinforce those of Jesus when he tells us that our body is a temple of the Holy Spirit. He believes this so firmly that he cannot accept that Christians would use their body for sin. Since we are temples of the Holy Spirit, every sin we commit is a sin against the body, which has been made sacred in Christ.

Several years ago a movie posed the question, *Whose body is it, anyway?* The answer for many is that it is MY body. Paul, however, would not agree with such an answer. According to Paul, our bodies are temples of the Holy Spirit, and to sin against our body is to sin against this sacred temple of the Holy Spirit. Paul's attitude about the body is certainly countercultural. He tells us that as temples of the Holy Spirit, we are not our own; our bodies belong to God. When someone says, "This is my body, and I have a right to do what I want with it," he or she is acting contrary to the Scriptures. These are deep and challenging words for us to ponder.

✠ *What can I learn from this passage?*

Day 3: Advice to the Married (7:1–24)

Paul speaks to the Corinthians concerning specific questions that have arisen within the community. We should not interpret Paul's words in this passage as a treatise on marriage. Some of the Corinthians believed they were no longer bound to their spouses after their baptism, while others believed marriage did not matter since it was the spirit and not the body that was important. They apparently saw marriage as something for the body. In answering the Corinthians, however, Paul speaks from the context of the Second Coming of Christ, which he expected to occur.

Because of the Second Coming of Christ, Paul teaches that one would be better off without any sexual relations, but if a person has a strong sexual need, then he or she should marry rather than commit sin. Through marriage, each one gives the other the right to their body, and neither the man nor the woman should reject this right unless they do so by mutual consent. Throughout this passage Paul treats women with much more concern than he would have learned from his Jewish background. During Paul's time, there was a Jewish practice of abstaining from sexual relations at a time of prayer (Exodus 19:15). Paul does not even allow this if one of the parties disagrees. Even when they do abstain for the sake of prayer, Paul urges them to continue their sexual relations after a time to avoid falling into sin. Paul seemed to imply that people entered into marriage because of their need for a sexual relationship; he makes no mention of the love that brings a man and a woman together.

Paul was apparently not married, and he wishes that all people had this gift. We must continue to keep in mind that Paul was speaking in the context of the imminent Second Coming of Christ. He wishes that all Christians could dedicate themselves to this preparation for the coming of Christ. Paul considers this a gift but admits that others have different gifts than he has. As he addresses the widows and those who are unmarried, he shares the same message with them. It would be better if they could remain unmarried, as he is, but he admits that it is better to marry than to live with a burning desire for sexual union.

Within Judaism during Paul's time, a woman was forbidden to divorce her husband, although she could apparently separate herself from him while continuing to live in the same house. Paul warns the woman who separates from her husband that she should live as a single person or seek reconciliation with her husband. The husband, as Christ himself had said, cannot divorce his wife. In preaching among those who were not Jewish, Paul found himself in the midst of unforeseen issues that were not treated in the Scriptures or in the words of Jesus. Within the Corinthian community, both wives and slaves owed allegiance to the man of the house, even to the point of choosing the same religion. Paul had to decide how to judge situations where one of the spouses accepted Christianity while the other remained a pagan.

Paul tells his readers that his decision comes from himself and not from the Lord. He directs the believer to remain with the unbeliever if the unbeliever does not object to the believer's practice of the faith. According to the common Jewish attitude at the time, the unbeliever would contaminate the believer, and therefore they should not remain together. Paul, however, takes an opposite view. He tells the believer to stay, and in this way the believer saves the unbeliever. This view was shared by many Christians at the time of Paul's letter to the Corinthians. Children born of Christian parents were considered holy, even if only one parent was Christian. It was also believed that if the unbeliever contaminated the believer, then he or she would also contaminate the child and make the child unholy. Paul, of course, rejects this attitude.

Paul views the call to marriage as a call to live in the peace of the Lord. If the unbeliever refuses to allow the believer to live in this peace, then the spouses may separate and are no longer bound to each other. Paul ends this passage on a more positive note, reminding the believing husband or wife that he or she could lead a spouse to conversion and salvation.

Furthermore, Paul calls those who believe that their baptism brought about external changes in their lives to continue living in the state in which they were baptized. He continues to write in the context that the Second Coming of Christ will take place soon. Paul tells his readers that this rule applies not only to them but to all the churches. Apparently some of those who were circumcised strove to have this condition reversed, while some who were not circumcised apparently believed that circumcision would make them more dedicated to their call. Paul tells both to leave things as they were at the time of their baptism. Circumcision or the lack of it has no value in Christianity. What really matters is how a person acts.

Paul gives the same message to slaves. He is not stating that slavery is good for society, but he is saying that baptism does not change that situation. Paul uses the idea of slavery and freedom to make a point. A slave is free in Christ, and a person who is free becomes a slave in Christ. The free person no longer belongs to himself or herself, but to Christ. Even if they gain freedom, slaves should still remember that they are slaves in Christ. During the time of Paul, slaves could buy freedom if they could earn enough money to do so. Paul refers to this idea when he speaks of the price paid for freedom in Christ. All have been "bought with a price"—namely, the death and resurrection of Jesus. Paul makes no mention of the one to whom this price is paid. He warns his readers not to return to the slavery of the wicked and repeats his admonition that all should continue in the state in which they were before their baptism.

Lectio Divina

Spend 8 to 10 minutes in silent contemplation of the following passage:

Some people believe that Paul was against marriage, but in reality, Paul wants those who are married and those who are single to remain faithful to their choice in life.

A certain medical missionary once had his plans set on marriage and settling down with his family in an affluent neighborhood. While traveling in a foreign country one day, he discovered people suffering unnecessarily from diseases eradicated in prospering countries centuries earlier. The suffering of the people touched him so deeply that he decided to abandon his plans for a more prosperous and softer life for a life in the jungles helping these people. He also decided he could not ask a wife to travel with him into such a life, so he took the vow of celibacy and dedicated himself to Christ and his ministry.

Another man who experienced a great desire to have a family met a woman who had the ideals and goals equal to his. They married, raised four children, and remained faithful in their dedication to the Lord. Throughout their marriage, they experienced many joys and difficulties, and in their prayers, they often had to call on the help of God to get them through some very difficult moments.

The reality of life is that the unmarried man in the jungle and the married couple had their difficult and joyful moments. When Paul speaks about marriage, he recognizes the challenge of not marrying and the commitment needed in marriage. He realizes that all people have a different calling and a different reason for choosing their direction in life. When Paul writes about marriage, he attempts to view it in the context of God's creation. Whether a person marries or not, the person must still remain faithful to one's choice in life.

✠ *What can I learn from this passage?*

Day 4: Paul's Views on Marriage (7:25–40)

In reading Paul's views on marriage, the reader should realize that he wrote in a different age to a particular people. He lived with the belief that the Second Coming of Christ would happen soon, and he experiences an urgency in helping the Corinthians to be prepared. His words should not be taken as his total teaching about marriage but only within the context of his belief that the Second Coming was about to happen. He begins by claiming that he has received no word from the Lord regarding virgins. What he writes here is his opinion about marriage and celibacy, which he admits comes from his own thoughts.

Paul tells those who are already married that they should remain in that state and not seek a separation. He believes it is better for those who are not married to remain in this state. For those who believe it would be sinful to marry after baptism, he instructs them that this is not so. He realistically recognizes that marriage has many trials, and Paul would like to help his readers avoid some of them. Since people are living in the last days and the time is near, they should keep their minds and hearts on the Lord and not be distracted by the needs of marriage or the world. In view of the Second Coming happening soon, he states that those who have a wife should act as though they do not have a wife. Those who are weeping, that is, living in difficulty, should live as though they are not facing these difficulties. Those who are rejoicing should live as though they are not rejoicing, and those who are using the world should act as though they are not using it. Paul's beliefs are driven by the thought that the world will soon end.

Paul's aim is to free people from the anxieties of the world. The unmarried man, free of family concerns, has more time to give to the Lord than the married, who must be concerned about the needs of his wife. The reason Paul continues to speak about this preference is that he truly believes he is urging his readers to a better form of preparation. He does not wish to burden his readers with stiff restrictions, but he wishes to offer them a means of devoting themselves more fully to the Lord. A woman who marries faces the same difficulties as the married man. A virgin, on the other hand, is anxious about the things of the Lord.

Writing in a male-dominated society, Paul speaks of a man's obligation toward his virgin. When Paul speaks of a man's virgin here, he appears to be speaking of a woman the man may or may not choose to marry, depending on the strength of the man's "passions." The man who marries is doing well, and the one who does not marry will do better. Paul recognizes the physical passion a man may feel, and he praises those of strong will who are able not to marry despite this passion. When Paul speaks of widows, he accepts the teaching that marriage binds a couple together as long as one's spouse is alive. In the case of a spouse's death, the living person may marry again, although Paul continues to advocate celibacy. Paul states that the widow who does marry should marry in the Lord. This could mean a marriage according to Christian customs or a marriage between Christian partners. Paul reiterates his belief that a widow would be better off if she remains as she is, that is, celibate.

Lectio Divina

Spend 8 to 10 minutes in silent contemplation of the following passage:

Paul wrote his letter in the context of the Second Coming of Christ, which he believed would happen soon. He realizes that marriage comes as a gift from God for the sake of creation, and the choice of not marrying can also come from God for the sake of one's desire to dedicate his or her life totally to Christ's mission on earth.

Many of the saints who chose religious life tell stories of the conflict they endured with their parents, who believed they were making a foolish choice. Their parents wanted grandchildren and could not imagine anyone going through life without a spouse. The reality is that God calls us all to different vocations in life, and God gives a person the strength and grace to live that vocation. The call people receive is for them alone, and they are foolish to judge that their manner of life is the only call. The call to marriage comes from God, and the call to a celibate life dedicated to Christ comes from God. Throughout history, the married and the celibate life can claim a number of holy and good people in their ranks.

Although Paul in this passage leans in the direction of celibacy for dedication to the Lord and allows that some people must marry for the sake of avoiding sin, the total message of the Scriptures points to the value of marriage and celibacy for the sake of fulfilling one's particular call. Both gifts come from God and are values in God's creation. The real challenge is not just a decision concerning one's direction in life, but the challenge of living faithfully in whatever vocation a person chooses to follow.

✠ *What can I learn from this passage?*

Review Questions

1. How would cutting a person off from the community lead to that person's salvation?

2. What are your thoughts about Paul's command not to associate with people who are immoral?

3. How does Paul's ideas about bringing someone to be judged by unbelievers compare with our practice concerning lawsuits today?

4. What is Paul's basic message about one's state in life?

5. What do you think of Paul's advice concerning celibacy? Marriage? How might Paul's message on marriage and celibacy also be applied to those living the single life?

Offerings to Idols

1 CORINTHIANS 8—11

For I received from the Lord what I also handed on to you, that the Lord Jesus, on the night he was handed over, took bread, and, after he had given thanks, broke it and said, "This is my body that is for you. Do this in remembrance of me." In the same way also the cup, after supper, saying, "This cup is the new covenant in my blood. Do this, as often as you drink it, in remembrance of me" (11:23–25).

Opening Prayer (SEE PAGE 18)

Context

Part 1: 1 Corinthians 8—9 Paul urges the church of God at Corinth to act with love and concern for others and to respect their consciences, even when they realize that some of their beliefs are false. They may eat meat sacrificed to idols, since false gods do not exist, but if eating this food will give scandal to the weak, then out of love, they should refrain from eating this food sacrificed to idols. Paul lists his rights as an apostle and reports that he did not demand the fulfillment of these rights, so likewise the Corinthians ought not to place an obstacle in the way of those seeking to live the faith. Paul declares that he is all things to all people, a Jew to the Jew, a Gentile to the Gentile, and a weak person to the weak.

Part 2: 1 Corinthians 10—11 Paul warns the Corinthians against becoming overconfident in their practice of the faith. He recalls events from the Israelites' journey through the desert during the Exodus and what happened to the people when they grumbled against God or worshiped false idols. He teaches that Christians participate in the Body and Blood of Christ in the Eucharist. Christians may eat food offered to false gods, since false gods do not exist. If people are present who are weak in faith and who may take scandal at Christians eating this food offered to idols, then Christians should refrain from eating this food. For Paul, everything is lawful, but not everything is beneficial. Paul speaks about the decorum of men and women during worship. This is followed by a short discussion on the attitude needed to celebrate the Eucharist. People should eat and drink at home rather than eating together and ignoring those present who have nothing. Jesus gave us his Body and Blood, and to eat this offering of Jesus unworthily will bring judgment upon the person who does so.

PART 1: GROUP STUDY (1 CORINTHIANS 8—9)

Read aloud 1 Corinthians 8—9.

8:1–13 Eating food sacrificed to idols

One of the difficulties faced by the people of Corinth was the custom of offering to idols all foods before they were brought to the market to be sold. Paul now addresses this issue, recognizing that the strong in faith know it is not sinful to eat meat offered to idols, since the gods to whom the meat is offered do not really exist. He warns them, however, that their knowledge could lead to pride. As Christians, they should act with love and not with a haughty and proud show of knowledge. Love builds the faith of another.

If Christians wish to show off their knowledge and, in doing so, give scandal to those weak in the faith, they are really showing their lack of knowledge concerning faith in Christ. The Christian is called to love God, and God will "know" that person. The word *know* is used here in the typical scriptural sense of loving in an intimate way. Paul is saying that God loves the Christian who acts with love. Those who have knowledge know that there is only one God and that false gods do not exist. Paul lists himself among those who have this knowledge. Since these false gods and lords do not exist, then food offered to them is offered to no one, and anyone can eat this food. There is one God, who is Father of all, and one Lord, Jesus Christ, through whom all are made and live.

The problem the Corinthians of strong faith must recognize is that not all have strong faith. Some new converts, who still believe that meats sacrificed to idols cannot be eaten without sin, would sin by partaking of these meats as they must act in accordance with their conscience. Eating in itself neither brings a person closer to God nor draws a person away from God. For the weak who believe it is sinful to eat food offered to idols, however, such an action can be sinful. The strong in faith must be careful not to eat this meat in front of the weak in faith lest they too eat this meat against their conscience and thus sin. Because of the knowledge of the strong in faith, the weak one falls. Christ died as much for the weak as for the strong, and to sin against the weak is to sin against Christ.

Paul recognizes that not all actions that are permitted can be freely performed. Love, not knowledge, becomes the principle according to which the Christian must act. Paul is willing to abstain completely from meat for the rest of his life if it is necessary to prevent another Christian from sinning.

9:1–18 Paul's rights as an apostle

Paul now launches into a discussion concerning his rights as an apostle. He builds on the theme in the previous passage, which speaks of a true disciple as one who, out of love for the community, does not always do those things that are permitted. Paul is apparently answering some questions concerning his call as an apostle. Since we do not know what those questions were, we can only guess what they might have been from the responses given by Paul.

Some of the Corinthians may have questioned Paul's apostleship because he did not act in the same manner as the other apostles. Through a series of questions, Paul is telling his readers that he acts freely, as an apostle who has seen the Lord. Whether he is an apostle to others is of no consequence, because he can point to the church at Corinth as the seal of his apostleship to them. For the Corinthians, Paul is an apostle of the Lord.

Paul is also telling those who have attacked him that he does, indeed, have rights—namely, to eat and drink all foods, to marry, and to receive support from those he serves, just as a soldier receives his wages, a keeper of the vineyard receives the fruit of the vineyard, and a shepherd receives milk from his flock. Paul names Barnabas, a companion mentioned in the Acts of the Apostles (11:19–26, 13:1–4), as one who also has these rights and who, like Paul, does not use them. Paul seems to realize that he may sound as if he is only concerned with material needs, so he reminds his readers that even Moses recognized these needs. Paul borrows a quotation from the Book of Deuteronomy (25:4), which states that the ox should not be muzzled while working. If an animal deserves this consideration, so an apostle should not be muzzled with material obligations while working. Those who plow and harvest seek a return for their labors. The apostle, who has sown the Spirit in the hearts of the Corinthians, certainly has a right to call on them for material support.

Other disciples have apparently received support from the Corinthians, and Paul does not dispute their rights to this support. He tells his readers, however, that he has an even greater right to their support, although he has never used it. In fact, Paul tells them that he has tolerated every type of difficulty so that they could never claim he was working for personal gain from this community. He wanted nothing to stand in the way of his preaching the gospel. He continues by using the example of those treated with the most respect within a community, those who give service in the temple and at the altar. Even these, he tells them, receive support in return. In the Old Testament, we read that the minister in the temple and at the altar has a right to receive sustenance from the offering (Numbers 18:30–32; Deuteronomy 18:1ff). Paul applies this command from the Lord to those who preach the gospel.

Paul states that he has not tried to make use of the rights he has and that, even more important, he is not looking for any return at this time. He gives his reason for not seeking any support, saying he would rather accept death than let anyone take away his right to boast. He admits he is so taken up with the gospel that he cannot boast about his preaching because it is such a strong compulsion for him. His willingness to preach the gospel is return enough, and if he preaches unwillingly, then he still recognizes his duty to preach. His need to preach, which he fulfills willingly, has as its source his call to stewardship. The return Paul seeks comes in knowing that he freely and willingly preaches the gospel without seeking the many rights that truly belong to the one who preaches.

9:19–27 All things to all

Paul no longer considers himself bound by the Jewish practices of the Mosaic Law, but despite his freedom in this and other areas, he is willing to live as a slave for the sake of leading as many people as possible to faith in Christ. Rather than live by his freedom and the knowledge that brought this freedom, Paul lives in love, allowing himself to act as a Jew bound by the law when in the company of those who believe this is necessary and acting as one free from the law when in the company of those who believe they are free. Earlier Paul stated that true knowledge is tempered by love and not pride (8:1–3). Paul declares that he is not totally free because he is subject to the Law of Christ. In the company of the weak, he is willing to be weak, and in the company of the strong, he is willing to be strong. For the sake of the gospel, as well as for the sake of bringing the weak to Christ, he has made himself all things to all people, conscious of the strength or weakness of the people whose company he shares.

Paul teaches his message by using an image from sports. In Paul's day, as in our own, sports were a popular form of entertainment. He states that just as a runner must discipline the body and keep his eye on the goal, so the follower of Christ must do the same. The followers of Christ must run and seek to win, which means they must be willing to endure all that is necessary to follow Christ. The runner in the Greek gymnasium seeks an award that eventually fades and perishes, but the Christian seeks eternal life, an award that will never perish. Paul is aware of the obstacles encountered in the struggle, both within the person and outside the person, and he tells his readers that his fight is a serious one. He does not run without a goal, and he does not engage in shadowboxing. Paul is telling the reader that his spiritual race is a real one. Like an athlete, he drives his body and trains it, fearing that in preaching to others, he himself may be disqualified. In other words, he drives himself for fear that in preaching to others he himself will not reach salvation.

Review Questions

1. Is it fair that Paul tells Christians not to eat meat sacrificed to idols when they do not believe that the false gods actually exist? Explain.
2. Why does Paul emphasize that he does not use his rights as an apostle?
3. How are Jesus' ministers compensated today for their work in the ministry?
4. Paul tells us that he is "all things to all." How might we follow his example in our lives today?

Closing Prayer (SEE PAGE 18)

Pray the closing prayer now or after *lectio divina*.

Lectio Divina (SEE PAGE 11)

Relax your body and maintain a posture of prayer (back straight, eyes shut, feet flat on the floor). This exercise can take as long as you want, but in the context of this Bible study, 10 to 20 minutes should be sufficient.

The meditations that follow are provided only to help group participants use this prayer form, but note that *lectio* is intended to bring one to a place of prayerful contemplation where the Word of God speaks to the hearer from his or her heart. (See page 11 for further instruction.)

Eating food sacrificed to idols (8:1–13)

Jesus said, "It is not what enters one's mouth that defiles that person; but what comes out of the mouth is what defiles one" (Matthew 15:11). Paul tells us to make sure that our freedom in believing we are allowed to perform some action does not become a stumbling block to the weak. Although he knows he can eat food sacrificed to false gods who do not exist, he does not eat such food to avoid scandalizing those who believe that eating this food is sinful.

A woman in a country where women were supposed to have their heads covered refused to cover her head, saying it was an insult to women to be told what to wear. A friend, however, urged her to follow the custom of the country, since she would not only offend the men of the town but also the women who felt a need to wear a head covering. The friend asked how the woman would feel if a man came into her house for an elegant dinner wearing a baseball cap, which he insisted on wearing during dinner. It would become a very uncomfortable situation for the other guests who came dressed for the elegant occasion. The woman agreed to wear a head covering.

Some may believe that swearing is not sinful, but swearing in front of someone who believes that swearing is an atrocious sin could cause scandal for the one who hears it. "Listen to that person swear! And he is a Catholic!" Love demands that we become conscious of the person who can become scandalized by the words or actions we may not consider sinful.

✠ *What can I learn from this passage?*

Paul's rights as an apostle (9:1–18)

As an apostle to the Corinthians, Paul has certain rights he does not use. For instance, he can call upon the Corinthians to provide food and drink for him, but he refuses to demand this right.

There is a humorous story about a grandmother who needed her lawn mowed by her grandsons, Mike and George. When Mike cuts her lawn, he always asks for the same payment that he charges others. George, however, refused to accept anything from his grandmother when he cut her lawn. After all, she was his grandmother. One day, the grandmother responded to Mike when he asked for payment, "Why can't you be like your brother? He is good for nothing."

Paul was good to the Corinthians for nothing. At times, we show kindness to family members, but as Christians, we are also called to show kindness to strangers or to someone in need. We act in this manner because Christians are called to love as Christ loved. Paul gave an example of such love when dealing with the Corinthians. One who acts with love for another in need because of Christ may have a right to compensation, but if the needy person cannot pay, Christians should never expect something in return.

✠ *What can I learn from this passage?*

All things to all (9:19–27)

Paul is inviting us to become all things to all people. To the Jews, he was a Jew; to the Gentiles, he became a Gentile; and to the weak, he became weak. Like Paul, we are to act with humility, always realizing that we are no better than those we serve. There are stories about Pope John XXIII who at times traveled outside his confines to speak with people he would meet in the streets. He did this so often that someone gave him the name "Johnny Walker." He was the Pope, but he believed that he was first a servant and companion to all of God's children.

In Matthew's Gospel, we read that Jesus and John the Baptist presented two different images of sharing God's message. God sent them so that God could become all things to all. John the Baptist lived among the people as an ascetic, living on food he found in the desert and wearing rough clothing. The religious leaders were scandalized that Jesus did not fast, calling him a sinner and a glutton. Jesus, in frustration, accuses them of closing their minds to God's gift. He says that his generation were "like children who sit in marketplaces and call to one another, 'We played the flute for you, but you did not dance, we sang a dirge but you did not mourn'" (11:16–17). Jesus came in joy and John came in camel's hair, and the religious leaders rejected them both. Together, Jesus and John came as all things to all and were rejected.

When it was time to rejoice and dance, Paul rejoiced in the Lord, and when it was time to mourn by suffering hardships, he mourned. He was a humble apostle who never saw himself as better than others. He was one with them.

✠ *What can I learn from this passage?*

PART 2: INDIVIDUAL STUDY (1 CORINTHIANS 10—11)

Day 1: Warning Against Overconfidence (10:1–13)

The story of the Israelites' journey across the desert during the Exodus was a well-known story for many people of Paul's day. Throughout the Old Testament, prophets spoke of the infidelity of the people of the Exodus and God's punishment. Paul now warns the Corinthians not to become proud and overconfident, and he points to the journey in the desert as a warning against this overconfidence. He notes that he does not want them to be unaware of the implications of the Exodus journey, stressing this important event. For Paul, the Exodus journey foreshadows many of the characteristics of the gift of baptism.

Paul speaks of the people of Israel passing through the sea under the protection of a cloud, which was the manner in which God was present among them (Exodus 13:21–22). God led the people of Israel through the great sea, which was the Red Sea (Exodus 14:21–22). Through this presence of God and the passing through the sea, the people of Israel were baptized "into Moses." It is difficult to understand exactly what Paul signified by this idea of being "baptized into Moses." Since Paul views the Exodus as a type of precursor for baptism, this may have been a reference to the life into which a person enters through baptism. For Paul, through the sacrament of baptism, a person is baptized into Christ.

The Israelites received manna to eat in the desert (Exodus 16:4–15) and water to drink (Exodus 17:1–7). Paul refers to this manna and water as "spiritual food" and "spiritual drink." By avoiding the name of the food and drink, Paul is able to make a connection with the Eucharist. The people in the desert received drink when Moses struck a rock. The Israelites referred to God as their rock, as found in Psalm 95 where we read, "Come, let us sing joyfully to the Lord; cry out to the rock of our salvation" (95:1). Despite the gifts they received in the desert, the Israelites rebelled against God, who in turn punished them for their rebellion (Numbers 14:10–25).

Paul states that the Lord allowed these things to happen to the Israelites during the Exodus as an example for them so that they will not become as evil as the Israelites became. He refers to a point in the Exodus journey where the people cast a golden calf as an image of God and the people "sat down to eat and drink, and rose up to revel" (Exodus 32:6). He draws another warning from an incident in the Book of Numbers in which an Israelite brought a woman who worshiped a foreign god into his tent. Because of this incident and the people's worship of false gods, twenty-four thousand people died from the plague, and the plague ended only when a son of Aaron killed the man who brought the woman into his tent (Numbers 25:1–9). He urges his listeners not to test Christ as the Israelites tempted God to the point that God sent poisonous serpents among them (Numbers 21:4–9) and eventually declared that the whole generation with the exception of Caleb and Joshua would not enter the Promised Land (Numbers 14:2–37).

Paul not only sees the events as a punishment for the people of the Exodus, but he also believes that they have been written down as an example and warning for future generations. When Paul speaks of his generation as the ones "upon whom the end of the ages has come" (1 Corinthians 10:11), he is referring to his own generation as the one toward which all of these events were moving. He warns against overconfidence, reminding them that God has not afflicted them with more difficulties than ordinarily happen to most people in the course of life. God, who is faithful, will not allow them to be tempted beyond their strength, and when trials do come, God will provide help for them.

Lectio Divina

Spend 8 to 10 minutes in silent contemplation of the following passage:

Paul warns the people not to grumble against the loving God because of life's difficulties. In a book intended to help people live a better life, a writer began with a single paragraph that contained only three words. The words simply stated that life is difficult. In our daily endeavors, we experience difficulties as well as joys.

There were two women who worked long hours in a nursing home. One complained about her patients, her staff, and her long hours. The other rejoiced that God allowed her to serve her patients under such difficult circumstances. For both, life was difficult, but what brought grumbling from one produced joy in the other.

No one escapes the difficulties life has to offer. Jesus, who is God, had a difficult life and a horrible death. Yet he showed that a life with a mission has joys and difficulties. God provides us with energy, an ability to show compassion, and the gift of faith, which enables us to realize the value of all we do. As Christians, we recognize that our work and life experiences come from the goodness of God. With faith in God, we have the ability to see a value in those difficult moments. Paul, who knows from experience that life is difficult, invites us to trust that God will provide the grace we need to bear all that we encounter.

✠ *What can I learn from this passage?*

Day 2: Warning Against Idolatry (10:14—11:1)

Paul speaks with concern for the Corinthians, for whom he expresses his love. He now addresses the issue of idolatry in eating and drinking. He alludes first to the celebration of the Eucharist. Since the cup that is blessed is a sharing in the Blood of Christ and the bread that is broken is a sharing in the Body of Christ, so a sharing in this one loaf makes all Christians who celebrate this Eucharist one with the body of Christ. The unity of Christians is a constant theme of Paul's theology.

Paul calls the Corinthians to consider the Israelites. The Israelites would make a sacrificial offering and leave a portion of the sacrifice on the altar to be burnt as an offering to God. A second portion of the offering would be for the priests, and a third would be taken by the one offering the animal for sacrifice. Those who ate this portion apart from the altar were considered to be sharing, through a family meal, in the altar (table) of sacrifice. This was known as a communion offering, since the eating of the offering put the participants in communion with one another and with God.

Paul applies the understanding of this custom to the practice of sacrificing to false gods, which he speaks of as an offering to demons. He recognizes that meat offered to false gods or idols is not really offered, since the false gods do not really exist. The offering, however, is evil, and in that sense it becomes an offering to demons. It is not a god who receives the offering, but a demon. Those who participate in this offering, like those who take part in the Israelite offering, participate in the altar of sacrifice. If the altar of sacrifice is evil, then those who eat this sacrifice take part in the altar of demons.

No one can take part in the cup and table of God (Eucharist) and the cup and table of demons at the same time. Paul asks if the Corinthians are provoking the Lord to jealous anger. The wrath of a jealous God is mentioned throughout the Old Testament. In the Book of Exodus, when God gives the Commandments to Moses, ordering the people not to worship false idols, God says, "For I, the LORD, your God, am a jealous God" (20:5). Paul warns the Corinthians that they should not provoke this wrath. Paul then challenges the overconfidence of the Corinthians. As proud as they are of their strong faith, they must realize that they are not stronger than God. Paul is likely speaking of eating the food offered to idols in a public gathering where they could give scandal to the weak of faith. He has already stated that there is no sin for those strong in faith to eat food offered to idols since the false gods do not exist, but this eating should be done in their homes where there is no danger of scandal.

Paul's message about being allowed to eat food offered to idols as long as no scandal is given leads to his discussion concerning what is lawful and what is right. Although the strong Christian realizes that all things are lawful, Paul points out that not all is good for the building up of the community. The guide for one's actions should not be the good of the person performing the action, but the good of one's neighbor. Food brought to the market can be eaten without any qualms of conscience. To enforce this statement, Paul quotes from Psalm 24:1, which declares that all on earth is good because it comes from the Lord.

For those who accept an invitation to eat with unbelievers, Paul suggests they eat whatever is served without any remorse of conscience. Paul is apparently referring to a private invitation to eat and not an official public meal. Even in this case, however, if someone points out that the food was offered to idols, then Christians should refrain from eating it out of concern for the faith of one's neighbor. Paul poses an obvious objection to his rule. He asks why the strong in faith should refrain from eating food provided by God. Why should the conscience of others have this authority over them? The reason lies on a deeper level. Christians live no longer for themselves but for Christ, and whatever they do, whether it be eating, drinking, or anything else, the first guide for their actions should not be their own conscience but the glory of God. Paul implies that this glory is given to God through concern for one's neighbor, whether Jew or Greek. Just as he allows the needs of others to become his guide, so he invites the Corinthians to follow his example as he follows the example of Christ.

Lectio Divina

Spend 8 to 10 minutes in silent contemplation of the following passage:

The gauge Paul uses for all his actions is the glory of God. Do his actions bring glory to God, or do they distract from the glory of God? In the world today, many use the same norms when they ask themselves, "What would Jesus do in this situation?" Paul lived in a world where many converts to Christianity were pagans who still held onto some pagan ideas. For the sake of Christ, Paul would avoid doing what he was allowed to do for the sake of those who would take scandal from his actions.

An ambassador to a pagan country learned the customs for eating and drinking used by the natives. He was not to drink before the king drank first, and he was not to eat before the king's entourage began to eat. On one occasion, however, the king and his entourage invited the ambassador to see the inside of their temple. As each one of the natives walked through the entrance, they would take a spoon of incense from a bowl and put it into a censor. The ambassador, a Catholic, knowing the gesture was meant to worship a false god that he knew did not exist, omitted the gesture for the sake of any Christians who would take offense at this.

Like Paul, the ambassador was willing to follow the customs of the country, but if it hinted at any form of scandal for those observing him, he would omit the action. Paul teaches us that there are times when we must consider the beliefs of others and refrain from certain actions to keep from scandalizing, even though we realize these actions are not sinful.

✠ *What can I learn from this passage?*

Day 3: Women's Headdress (11:2–16)

Paul begins this passage by praising the Corinthians for their remembrance of him and his teachings. In this praise, he is acknowledging that they recognize him as one who teaches with authority. He addresses the need for proper decorum in liturgical worship, and he most likely is answering some problems raised by the Corinthians. Unfortunately, we do not know what exact issues Paul was addressing, and we can only guess at them as we read his response.

Paul recalls the order of creation as found in the Book of Genesis when he declares that the head of Christ is God, the head of man is Christ, and the head of woman is man. Much of what Paul has to say could be strongly influenced by the social attitudes of the time in which he lived and his Jewish background. He is not establishing new rules, but reminding the people of the rules of decorum in worship as understood in his day.

While at worship, a man should not cover his head because he is the image of God, and the glory of Christ should shine forth from him. The woman, however, should keep her head covered when she prays or prophesies, since she is a reflection of the man's glory. In some pagan areas, a woman who removed her veil was sending a sexual invitation to someone. For Paul, a woman without a veil has already consented in her mind to some sexual sin and thus is guilty of adultery. As a product of his own time and culture, Paul has no doubt that a woman should wear a veil.

Paul recalls from the Book of Genesis that a woman was made from a man (2:21), and not a man from a woman. Once this order was accepted, one must admit that the woman ought to wear some symbol of submission to the man, namely, the head covering. Some current commentators believe the story of creation does not show the submission of the woman, but the equality, since the story tells us that she was taken from the rib of the man and not created from the ground as the animals were (2:19). Following the story of creation of the first man and woman, Paul states that the man was not created for the woman, but the woman was created for the man as a companion, not as one subservient to him. The woman was created because it was not good for the man to be alone, and animals did not offer him suitable companionship (Genesis 2:18–25).

He states things that seem to change the meaning of some of the impressions given earlier. Neither the man nor the woman is independent of each other. Just as a woman came from a man, so now the man is born from woman, and all comes from God. When Paul speaks about one being the head of the other in the early portion of this passage, he now seems to mean the order of coming into being rather than one being greater than the other. Christ comes forth from the Father, the man comes forth from Christ, the woman comes forth from man, and all come forth from God. Without any knowledge of the question Paul is answering, it is difficult to know the exact message he wishes to share with his readers.

Although Paul seems to accept equality between the man and woman, he also adheres to the customs of the day. He asks his readers to judge how people should act in worship. He asks the question not to find an answer, but because the answer seems obvious. Women, according to custom, should wear a veil and long hair, while men should wear their hair short. For a woman to cut her hair short or a man to wear long hair would, in Paul's estimation, imply that one wishes to be like the opposite sex. For those who wish to argue this point, Paul simply states that all the churches recognize the manner of decorum stated in this passage.

Lectio Divina

Spend 8 to 10 minutes in silent contemplation of the following passage:

In presenting his message about proper decorum during worship, Paul is challenging cultural attitudes on the one hand while following them on the other. It is as though he is following his previous teaching that everything is lawful but not everything builds up the community.

In the Gospel of Luke, we read the story of Jesus' visit to Martha and Mary. In the story, Mary is sitting at the feet of Jesus, and Martha complains that she has to do all the work while Mary sits listening to Jesus. Jesus responds that Mary "has chosen the better part and it will not be taken from her" (10:42). In this remarkable story, Jesus and Mary are acting contrary to culture. In Jesus' day, a woman dared not sit at the feet of a rabbi to learn, but Mary defies this custom, and Jesus praises her for it.

Just as Jesus showed concern for the rights of all people, he chose to teach a new message about the place of women in society. He taught that men and women have an equal role in God's creation. Paul stresses this reality when he notes that men and women take part in creation. He states that the woman came from the man and a man is born from the woman. Both have a deep, unified relationship with the other. In the end, all things come from God.

✠ *What can I learn from this passage?*

Day 4: Celebrating the Lord's Supper (11:17–34)

Paul addresses the eucharistic gathering at Corinth. He does not praise the Corinthians for celebrating the Eucharist, but he corrects them and teaches the true meaning of the eucharistic celebration. He notes that the eucharistic celebration, which should be a matter of spiritual growth for the Corinthians, becomes a matter of spiritual harm. Paul has received reports of factions existing in the celebration of the Eucharist. Since he has already heard about the problems within the Corinthian church, he states that he has no trouble believing these reports. He wonders if these factions must continue to exist to allow the strong in faith to stand out above the others. In any event, Paul tells the Corinthians that they cannot claim they are gathering to celebrate the Lord's Supper, because their actions do not coincide with the love central to this celebration. Some eat and get drunk while others go hungry. Instead of receiving a share from those who have food and drink, the poor who have nothing suffer embarrassment. Paul asks the people if they lack homes where they can eat and drink. If they eat and drink in their homes, they can then gather together, not to eat and drink to their condemnation, but to celebrate the Lord's Supper. Otherwise, he finds no reason to praise them in their manner of gathering for the celebration.

After this rebuke, Paul shares a lesson concerning the celebration of the Lord's Supper and its meaning for those who gather. He declares that he passes on to them what he has received from the Lord, but he is most likely referring to the manner of celebration used by the early community. The community, faithful to the Lord, has passed this teaching on to him.

The manner of celebrating the Eucharist closely follows that found in the Gospel of Luke (22:15–20). Paul's version differs from the account in the Gospel of Luke by twice repeating Jesus' words, "Do this in remembrance of me." This is most likely an addition made by Paul, since it is not found in the early celebrations of the Eucharist.

Paul tells the Corinthians that the Lord took bread, gave thanks, broke it, and said, "This is my body that is for you. Do this in remembrance of me." Taking the cup, Jesus said, "This cup is the new covenant in my blood. Do this, as often as you drink it, in remembrance of me." The Corinthians may have understood the celebration of the Lord's Supper only as a memorial. Paul tells them that they actually share—that they proclaim by their words and actions—the death of the Lord until his Second Coming. Because this is so, those who share in this bread and cup unworthily are guilty of sinning against the Body and Blood of Christ.

Paul advises his readers to review their lives closely before sharing in this great gift. They should be conscious of the body of the Lord in each member of the community before sharing in the bread and cup or they will bring condemnation on themselves. The Jews believed that those who were sick or died prematurely were being punished by God. Paul, apparently alluding to this belief, gives the sinfulness of the Corinthians at the Lord's Supper as a reason for the sickness, disease, and death in their midst. This could be avoided if they examined their lives closely, but as it is, God punishes them to cleanse them from their sinful ways.

Paul ends by reminding his readers that they should show concern for one another in sharing the Lord's Supper, waiting patiently for one another and eating at home if they are hungry. In this way, their gathering becomes a cause for praise and not for condemnation. The Corinthians have apparently sought Paul's guidance on other issues about the Lord's Supper, but Paul defers any comment until he visits with them.

Lectio Divina

Spend 8 to 10 minutes in silent contemplation of the following passage:

Paul links the offering of Jesus' Body and Blood in the Eucharist to love within the community. Those who believe they are sharing in the Eucharist without being concerned for one's neighbor do not understand the full significance of this gift.

A man wrote a story about an ordained priest he met in a concentration camp who secretly received a small amount of wine smuggled in for the celebration of the Eucharist for those confined in his barracks. When he received his daily ration of bread earlier in the day, he kept it for the celebration. Before he celebrated the Eucharist, he would share some of his bread with others in the camp, despite his own hunger. He kept aside only enough to celebrate the Eucharist. He considered the sharing of his bread as his spiritual preparation for the celebration of the Eucharist. Paul the Apostle would have applauded this man for his understanding of the Eucharist as a celebration of love between Christ and the one celebrating, and between every person in the community taking part in the celebration.

The reality of celebrating the Eucharist as taught by Paul is that taking part in the eucharistic celebration demands more than being present. It demands action and concern for the poor, for the suffering, for those who need support. Love of God and neighbor and not just attendance alone makes the celebration of the Eucharist meaningful. Paul is not only speaking about the actions and words of Jesus at the Last Supper, but he is reminding the Corinthians of the underlying message of Jesus' love in giving his Body and Blood. For Paul, celebrating the Eucharist is not only celebrating the love of Jesus for all people, but it is the call to those celebrating to be willing to love one another.

✠ *What can I learn from this passage?*

Review Questions

1. What warnings would Paul have for us today as he draws lessons from the Exodus story?

2. What does Paul mean when he says that everything is lawful?

3. Why are women today exempt from wearing head coverings to worship when Paul tells us that women should have their head veiled?

4. We can trace some of the theology of the Eucharist as a meal and a sacrifice to these passages in 1 Corinthians. Discuss Paul's theology of the Eucharist found in these Scripture passages.

5. How can you prepare to celebrate the Eucharist well?

Spiritual Gifts

1 CORINTHIANS 12—16

If I speak in human and angelic tongues, but do not have love, I am a resounding gong or a clashing cymbal. And if I have the gift of prophecy and comprehend all mysteries and all knowledge; if I have all faith so as to move mountains, but do not have love, I am nothing (13:1–2).

Opening Prayer (SEE PAGE 18)

Context

Part 1: 1 Corinthians 12—14:19 Paul speaks of the gifts that come to us through the action of the Holy Spirit. All gifts are given for the common good. There are a variety of gifts, but their source is the same Spirit, Lord, and God. The gifts include wisdom and the ability to share this wisdom, healing, performing great deeds, prophesying, discernment of spirits, speaking in tongues, and interpretation of tongues. Just as a body has many parts, so the Church has many parts, that is, many gifts that enable the Church to function as the body of Christ on earth. Each person in the community shares in at least one of these gifts. The foundation for the use of all gifts is love, which is the greatest of all virtues. Without love, all that a person does is empty and futile. Paul mentions that he prefers that people have the gift of prophecy, since prophecy is directed toward building up the community.

Part 2: 1 Corinthians 14:20—16 Among the gifts of the Spirit received by the Corinthians is the gift of speaking in unknown tongues. Paul would rather have people prophesy than to speak in tongues, since speaking in tongues is a form of praise that exists between the one who prays in tongues and God and that is prayed in a manner unintelligible to most. Paul would rather the gift of prophecy be given, since it teaches a message that is understood by all present. When one speaks in tongues, Paul seeks someone to interpret the tongues for the community. After he establishes an order for the use of the gifts of the Spirit, he teaches about resurrection from the dead.

If Christ is preached as raised from the dead, then no one can deny that there is a resurrection. Resurrection is different from our existence here on earth. It is a spiritual existence. Paul ends by speaking of a collection to be brought to the church at Jerusalem and adds a note about his travel plans. He ends his letter by sending greetings to the church at Corinth from himself and others.

PART 1: GROUP STUDY (1 CORINTHIANS 12—14:19)

Read aloud 1 Corinthians 12—14:19.

12:1–11 Many gifts, but one God

Although the Corinthians can claim many special gifts from the Spirit, Paul wishes to help them properly discern these gifts. According to Paul, the Corinthians have some mistaken notions that must be corrected. He reminds his readers that they were led astray by mute idols during the time they were pagans. Although these idols did not actually exist, belief in them had a special hold over the Corinthians. Just as they came to false conclusions concerning the power of the mute idols, so also could they come to false conclusions about the work of the Spirit in their midst. The Holy Spirit, Paul tells them, leads them to proclaim faith in Jesus as the Lord. Those who turn against Jesus are actually cursing Jesus, and they are not led by the Spirit. Paul may be referring to those who accept faith in Christ but who are also following the Judaizers in accepting the Mosaic practices. In rejecting this freedom that comes from Christ, they are, in effect, rejecting Christ.

Although Christians share in a diversity of gifts and services, Paul reminds them that there is one God, whom he names as Spirit, Lord, and God. Although there are different gifts, there is one Spirit; different forms of service, but one and the same Lord; and different works, but the one God who produces them in everyone. Just as there is unity in God, so all gifts, although diverse, work toward the one goal. Each person has specific gifts, given not for himself or herself alone, but for the good of the community. Paul names some of these gifts.

Some are able to express knowledge by teaching God's message. Some have a gift of deep faith, others are able to perform healings through the action of the Spirit, and others are able to perform great deeds in the Spirit. Some have the gift of prophecy, which is the gift of being able to proclaim God's Word. Others have the ability to discern spirits, which enables them to determine whether one's inner experiences come from the Spirit. Some have the gift of speaking in tongues, which refers to the ability of praising God in unintelligible sounds that fill a person with a deep experience of God's presence. The ability to interpret tongues comes to the person who shares with the community a message flowing from those who pray in tongues.

The gift of tongues, possibly because of its mysterious manifestation, seemed to be the highly valued gift among the Corinthians. They had just moved from the Greek mystery cults and magic of the paganism of their day, so the act of praying in unintelligible sounds appealed to them. Lest anyone feel that any specific gift places one above another, Paul teaches that the one and same Spirit is responsible for these different gifts, sharing them according to the needs of the community.

12:12–31a One body, many parts

In an earlier passage, Paul challenged the Corinthians' ideas concerning the body. Some believed that the deeds performed by the body had nothing to do with the spirit and that one could do whatever he or she wished with the body. Paul now uses the idea of the body in a different sense, expressing the body's need for each of its members and applying this idea to Christians as the body of Christ. He recognizes that the Church has members with many different gifts, and he wishes to teach that all gifts work together for the good of the entire community. Like a single body made up of many members, Paul sees the Christian community as the body of Christ, composed of many members. Through the gift of baptism in the one Spirit, all people, Jews and Greeks, slaves and free, have become one with the body. Paul uses an image of all drinking of the one Spirit, an image that some commentators believe points to the Eucharist. Many others, however, believe Paul is referring to baptism.

Paul continues to use the image of the body to show the importance of each member in the community. Although the body is one, it consists of many members working together. A foot could not say it does not belong to the body because it is not a hand, just as an ear could not say it does not belong to the body because it is not an eye. If the whole body were an eye, how would a person hear? All members of the body, although they have different functions, are important to the body as a whole. If all the Corinthians had the same gifts, they would be like a body that is all eye or all ear. It would not be a functioning body because it would lack the other needed gifts. The eye cannot say it does not need the hand, and the head cannot say it does not need the feet. Just as one part of the body cannot say it does not need another part, so the Corinthians cannot deny their need for different gifts within the community.

Some parts of the body could be considered less important or less honorable than others, but they often receive more care. This may be a reference to the Corinthians' idea that the physical body is less important than a person's spiritual gifts. Within the community, there are those considered less honorable, but God has given them greater gifts. Paul continues to address the divisions taking place within the Corinthian community. Because all members of the body need one another to function as a healthy unit, all suffer with the suffering members and all rejoice with the honored members.

Paul tells the Corinthians that they all belong to the body of Christ. Within this body exists an order of importance. First in line are the apostles, the shapers of the community. Paul is not referring here to the Twelve, but to people such as himself who preach the gospel for the sake of establishing or building up the community. Next in line are the prophets who speak in the name of God. Then come the teachers, those who continue to explain the gospel to the members of the community. Behind them comes everyone from those who perform miracles to those who speak in tongues. Because the Corinthians placed so much stress on the ability to speak in tongues, Paul places it at the end of his list of gifts, as though he considers this the least of the gifts. Just as a body is not all eye or all ear, so Paul reminds the members of the Corinthian community that they are not all apostles or prophets or teachers or possessors of all the other gifts. Instead of seeking these gifts, they should desire the greater gifts, which we will soon discover are the gifts used with love.

12:31b—13 The importance of love

The passage on love moves away from the point of Paul's letter and may have been an independent letter written by Paul that is incorporated by an editor into this letter. Linking this passage with the letter, an editor could easily apply the message as a solution to the divisions in the Corinthian community. The passage itself is highly poetical and one of the most widely quoted of all Paul's letters. Paul tells the church of God at Corinth that, without love, those with an abundance of gifts, even if they sound more angelic than human, would be no better than a dull, clanging cymbal. Those with the exalted gifts of prophecy, knowledge, or deep faith would be nothing without love. Even those who feed the poor and accept martyrdom are nothing without love. The Corinthians have cultivated many gifts, but Paul views them as lacking the spirit that enlivens these gifts, namely, love.

In a community filled with bickering and pride, Paul offers love as a solution to their problems. The Corinthians have a need for love that is patient and kind, without any signs of jealousy, arrogance, boastfulness, rudeness, selfishness, anger, or resentfulness. Love rejoices with the truth, not in wrongdoing. Paul recognizes that true love does not put limits on its gift. It bears all, believes all, hopes all, and endures all. Gifts such as prophecy, knowledge, and speaking in tongues will cease because they are imperfect. They are partial gifts. Love, however, will never cease. When the day of fulfillment comes, the imperfect will pass away.

Paul notes that when he was a child, he did those things that were childish, but when he became an adult, he put aside his childish ways. Just as a child's understanding develops as the child grows into adulthood, so we will eventually understand all. Our understanding of God and creation is imperfect, and our vision is clouded, as though we are looking in a mirror. The point will come when we will see God face to face, and all will become clear. Our imperfect knowledge will reach perfection. For the Corinthians who placed so much value on knowledge, this was an important message. When all is ended, only faith, hope, and love will endure, and of these three, the greatest is love. The Church refers to the virtues of faith, hope, and love as "theological virtues" and teaches Paul's message that love is the greatest of the three.

14:1–19 Prophecy and speaking in tongues

Having emphasized the importance of the gift of love, Paul urges the Corinthians to seek this love and to allow it to guide them in the use of the spiritual gifts they have received. The gift he sees as fulfilling this demand for love is the gift of prophecy, because it is directed toward building up the community and the encouraging of others in faith. In the Scriptures, the gift of prophecy does not refer to predicting the future, but to speaking God's message. Those who preach or teach share in the gift of prophecy.

Although the Corinthians believed speaking in tongues was the greatest gift, Paul teaches that the greatest of all gifts is the gift of prophecy. The one praying in tongues is speaking with God and not with the community; no one profits from this gift except the one praying in tongues. It is a form of prayer that draws the person speaking in unknown tongues to a deeper experience of God's presence. Although Paul would like everyone in the community to speak in tongues, he would rather they receive the gift of prophecy. The only exception Paul gives to this is the person who can interpret tongues. This person, like the prophet, uses this gift for the building up of the community.

Paul realizes that he has established the community at Corinth through his preaching of the gospel. He asks the Corinthians what would have happened if he had come to them speaking only in tongues. They were in need of revelation, knowledge, prophecy, and teaching. Even music needs some order to its sound to convey a distinguishable tune. A bugle needs a distinctive sound to call soldiers to battle. A person speaking in tongues might as well be speaking to empty space, because those listening cannot understand the sounds he or she is making. Paul further draws an image from language itself, saying that a person who speaks a foreign language cannot be understood and is therefore not able to share a message with the people being addressed. Because the Corinthians are so intent on sharing in spiritual gifts, Paul urges them to seek an abundance of those gifts that build up the Church.

According to Paul's thinking, the one who prays in tongues should pray for the gift of interpreting tongues. The Greeks often separated the person into spirit and mind, seeing the mind as closer to the physical body than the spirit. Because some of the Corinthians, influenced by Greek thinking, thought little of the body, this prayer with the spirit alone appealed to them. Paul declares he would rather pray and sing with the spirit and the mind. When people heard a prayer they accepted, they would proclaim their agreement by adding the final "Amen." If those listening to the one praying did not understand what he or she was saying, they would not be able to state their "Amen." The praise of God is present, but no one is able to understand it.

Paul apparently possessed many of the gifts of the Spirit, and here he states that he himself speaks in tongues. If he had to make a choice, however, he would choose the ability to utter a few words of prophecy over the ability to pray a countless number of words in tongues.

Review Questions

1. What message about the Church as a community in Christ do we receive when Paul says there is unity in diversity?
2. What gifts has the Holy Spirit granted you?
3. How important are we to God's plan for creation? Share some insights.
4. Are people able to perform good acts without love? Explain.
5. What is your understanding of the gift of tongues?
6. What spiritual gift would you prefer to be given to build up the community?

Closing Prayer (SEE PAGE 18)

Pray the closing prayer now or after *lectio divina*.

Lectio Divina (SEE PAGE 11)

Relax your body and maintain a posture of prayer (back straight, eyes shut, feet flat on the floor). This exercise can take as long as you want, but in the context of this Bible study, 10 to 20 minutes should be sufficient.

The meditations that follow are provided only to help group participants use this prayer form, but note that *lectio* is intended to bring one to a place of prayerful contemplation where the Word of God speaks to the hearer from his or her heart. (See page 11 for further instruction.)

Many gifts, but one God (12:1–11)

Paul reminds us that there are different gifts, but one and the same Spirit responsible for giving these gifts. Instead of taking pride in our gifts, we must realize they come from God for the common good.

The Book of Numbers (22:22–35) has an amusing story about a talking donkey. Balaam, a prophet who is hired to curse the Israelites, sets out to fulfill his mission. At one point, the donkey sees an angel blocking the path, but Balaam does not see the angel. When the donkey refuses to move on, Balaam beats the donkey. This happens three times, and it ends when the donkey speaks, asking Balaam why he is beating her.

When Balaam sees the angel, he learns that if the donkey had moved on despite seeing the angel on the path, Balaam would have died. Balaam learned his lesson from a talking donkey. God is in control, and if God does not wish for Balaam to curse the Israelites, he will not be able to do it.

At the beginning of a retreat, the retreat director told his audience that if God can use a talking donkey to convey a message to Balaam, then God can use him to convey a message to them. The retreat director was teaching that whatever we do with our life, we do because God enables us to do it. By the grace of God, we are able to perform good deeds because we have received a special gift given for the common good of creation. It is foolish to believe we can perform good acts that affect the lives of others without God's help. Balaam eventually praises the Israelites, which is what the Lord wants him to do. Christians realize that God's gifts are meant in the end to praise God.

✠ *What can I learn from this passage?*

One body, many parts (12:12–31a)

Paul stresses that the human body, although it has many parts, is one body. It is the same with the body of Christ on earth. There are many parts, but just one body of Christ.

As we read the history of the saints in the Church, we recognize they all served the same Lord, yet they did it in a variety of ways. Saint Teresa of Avila reformed the Carmelites, while Saint Ignatius of Loyola founded a missionary order. Saint Thomas Aquinas developed a theological foundation for teaching truths of the Church, while Saint Francis of Assisi founded the Franciscans and traveled far and wide to share God's message. In our own era, Blessed Teresa of Calcutta spent the major part of her life tending the needs of poor people in remote areas, while Pope John Paul II traveled throughout the world to spread the message of the Church.

In our neighborhoods, we have those who teach, those who participate in the eucharistic liturgy daily, those who work among the poor, those who raise families dedicated to Christ, those who fix up homes and mow lawns for the elderly, and those who accept the pain and disappointments of life for the love of Christ. The gifts, different as they are, come to us through the action of the Holy Spirit. There are many gifts, but one body. Every day, the body of Christ walks, works, prays, and suffers on this earth. This is our faith. We are proud to profess it in Christ Jesus, our Lord.

✠ *What can I learn from this passage?*

The importance of love (12:31b—13)

Paul is delivering a similar message when he tells us that love should be the motive for all we do. A man running for public office made a large donation to a soup kitchen, but he wanted a picture in the newspaper showing him handing the check to the one managing the kitchen. Another man shocked members of the Salvation Army each Christmas when they opened their bucket to find a large sum of money squeezed into a small envelope in the bucket. This man made his donation quietly and without any special recognition.

One Christmas, someone caught him dropping his envelope into the bucket and asked him why he hid his identity. His answer was that he saw how the poor were so hungry and in such need that he felt a deep compassion and love for them in their plight. For him, the important thing was that the poor would be fed, not that he received praise for his donation. He said, "I'll leave the reward up to God."

Jesus said, "When you give alms, do not blow a trumpet before you, as the hypocrites do in the synagogues and in the streets to win the praise of others. Amen, I say to you, they have received their reward" (Matthew 6:2). The action of the man who wanted his picture in the paper to receive recognition was blowing a trumpet in his own way, acting out of self-concern rather than out of love. In the eyes of God, he already received his reward. The man who had concern for the poor rather than for receiving the praise of others was acting more like Jesus. Love is the greatest of all virtues. "Love never fails" (1 Corinthians 13:8).

✠ *What can I learn from this passage?*

Prophecy and speaking in tongues (14:1–19)

The gift of praising God in unknown tongues was a gift shared by many of the Corinthians. As great as the gift was, Paul declared he would rather people use the gift of prophecy, that is, speaking about God in a manner that would touch their hearts and lead them to a life closer to Christ.

A pastor who prayed with a group dedicated to the Holy Spirit would speak in tongues during prayer meetings. When he preached on weekends, the parishioners reported that his message always enriched them spiritually. He lived close to the Lord, prayed often, and had a special dedication to reading and praying with the Scriptures. Like Paul the Apostle, he had the gift of tongues and the gift of prophecy, and he used them wisely. He prayed in tongues in prayer groups and touched hearts with the gift of prophecy when he preached.

Although many of us do not have the gift of praising God in unfamiliar tongues, we have the gift of being able to pray and ask the Lord to speak through us when necessary. The gift of prophecy (sharing the Word of the Lord) is a great gift that all people may receive at some point in life. It may express itself in a healing or encouraging word or in an explicit reference to the Scriptures. It expresses itself in those who teach religion to children or in those who share a thought in a study group.

Through the gift of the Holy Spirit, we are able to touch the hearts of those we encounter. To presume that we can preach or teach in the Lord's name demands that we remain faithful to God through prayer. Paul wishes that all could speak in tongues, but for those who do not, Paul recognizes the need for all people to be people of prayer.

✠ *What can I learn from this passage?*

PART 2: INDIVIDUAL STUDY (1 CORINTHIANS 14:20—16)

Day 1: Warning Against Overconfidence (14:20–40)

Paul warns the Corinthians not to act with the immaturity of children in their attitude toward these gifts. They should have the innocence of children to keep them from evil, and the true use of these spiritual gifts demands maturity. Paul cites a quotation from Isaiah (28:11) in which God speaks of using a strange language to speak with the people of Israel. This strange language refers to the language of the invaders, which the Israelites did not understand at the time when foreign nations invaded Israel. In adapting this quotation to the situation, Paul changes it slightly, applying it to the unbelievers who, like the Corinthians, become easily impressed with the magic of speaking in tongues. Prophecy, however, enables a person to understand what is being said and to deepen his or her faith.

Because the gift of tongues profits only the one using it, the unbeliever who enters an assembly of people praying in tongues would think the members of the assembly had lost their minds. Just as the Israelites linked the foreign tongues with the pagan invaders, so the unbelievers would link the praying in tongues with some type of pagan ritual. The gift of prophecy, however, will challenge the unbeliever or the new Christian, who will openly proclaim the presence of Christ in the midst of the assembly.

Because of their flair for emphasizing the gifts, the Corinthians apparently vied with one another in the use of these gifts during worship. Instead of praying in an orderly fashion, they competed with one another in a desire to show off their particular gifts. Paul calls for order and self-restraint when the assembly gathers. He suggests the service include psalm prayers, instructions, revelations, and speaking in tongues as long as someone is there to interpret. The experience should lead to the building up of the community. If an interpreter is not present, then those who speak in tongues should remain silent.

Even in sharing the gift of prophecy, Paul calls for order. If a person receives a revelation, then all should allow that person to speak, even if someone else was prepared to speak next. The spirit of prophecy does not overwhelm prophets to the point of possessing them. Prophets still have control over the prophecy, and they can wait their turn. Paul bases his reasoning on his belief in God as a God of order and peace, and not a God of confusion. A well-ordered assembly becomes a sign of God's presence.

In speaking of order in the assembly, the letter turns sharply to the topic of the place of women in the assembly. The change is so abrupt that many commentators believe the passage did not originally belong to this letter but was the work of a later writer. Some of the directions given here do not agree with Paul's earlier directive concerning women at worship. The passage calls for women to remain silent at worship, to be totally submissive, and to save any questions until they are at home where their husbands can instruct them. The passage harshly orders women not to shame the assembly by speaking out in church.

Paul returns to the topic of the true prophet who is able to recognize the truth of his words as coming from the Lord. Those who do not accept Paul's words should not be heard, because by ignoring his words, they show they do not have the true spirit of prophecy. As a final word on the subject, Paul again urges them to seek the spirit of prophecy but not to deny those who speak in tongues the opportunity to do so in an orderly manner.

Lectio Divina

Spend 8 to 10 minutes in silent contemplation of the following passage:

Paul realized that the Spirit bestowed many gifts on those who were baptized, but the gifts should be used in an orderly fashion for the sake of worship. Worship is not meant to be a cacophony of people speaking at the same time, but an order of worship that instructs, inspires, and enables true worship of God. It enables a community to praise God in word and song.

In the Roman Catholic Church, the name given to the sacrament of ordination into the order of presbyters (ordained priests) is the sacrament of holy orders. The name not only refers to the entry into the order of presbyters, but it also signifies that the ordained priest is also committed to holy order in worship. The ordained priest is the presider at liturgy, the one who enables the community to praise God with one heart and one voice.

Paul affirms that everyone should use the gifts given by the Holy Spirit, and the use of these gifts demands that they be used in an orderly fashion. Since the body of Christ worships God with one voice and one heart, Paul speaks of the value of order in worship. The body of Christ praises God in the one voice of the community at worship. When a child or adult celebrates the sacrament of baptism, the presider declares, "The Christian community welcomes you with great joy!" The newly baptized is welcomed into a community that raises a unified voice to God in the liturgy.

✠ *What can I learn from this passage?*

Day 2: The Appearances of Christ (15:1–11)

Paul calls the Corinthians to remember the gospel he preached to them, a gospel that not only teaches the Good News about Jesus but also has the power to bring salvation to those who remain firm in the faith. If they have changed this gospel in any way, they will have believed in vain. The gospel Paul shared with the Corinthians was not one he himself witnessed, but one he received from others. In these verses, he passes on the short creed he has received—namely, that Jesus died for our sins as the Scriptures foretold, that he was buried, and that in accordance with the Scriptures, he was raised on the third day. In Jewish thought, the number three was significant. The ancients used the number three to establish that something definitively happened. The message that Jesus was raised on the third day tells us that Jesus was truly dead before his resurrection.

Paul lists the witnesses to the resurrection of Jesus, which includes Cephas (Peter), the Twelve, five hundred disciples at once (symbolizing a large number of followers, some of whom were dead at the time Paul wrote this letter), James (the head of the church at Jerusalem, not James, one of the Twelve), the apostles (early preachers), and finally Paul. According to the Acts of the Apostles (9:1–9), Paul received his vision of the resurrected Christ on the road to Damascus, the town toward which he was traveling with the intention of arresting and persecuting Christ's followers. Paul identifies his call as a true gift from God, since he was performing deeds that deserved God's punishment rather than his gift. Because of this, he speaks of himself as an apostle born "abnormally." With the confidence of someone who knows he has done his best, Paul is able to declare that God's trust has not been given in vain. Paul is able to declare that with God's help, he has worked harder than all the rest. He exhorts that it does not matter whether the Corinthians have received the message from him or others. The important thing is the message they are preaching. Paul may be defending his right to preach about the resurrection of Christ.

Lectio Divina

Spend 8 to 10 minutes in silent contemplation of the following passage:

Paul the Apostle received a call to follow Christ after years of rejecting him. He referred to his early life as a waste. All his dedication to eradicating the followers of Christ were years he wasted on a useless mission. When he converted to Christ, his mission became meaningful.

Saint Augustine, who eventually became a bishop, lived a sinful life before his conversion. As gifted as he was, he would consider his early years as wasted on selfish pursuits. He had a child out of wedlock by a woman he knew and truly loved for eleven years. Augustine developed a desire to accept the Lord but felt that his old life of sin had a grip on him. He planned to marry into a respectable family, but he was unfaithful to his fiancée and chose another female companion for a period of time.

One day, agonizing in tears over his desire to serve the Lord, he heard children chanting, "Take and read," and he opened his Bible and read the lines that said "not in orgies and drunkenness, not in promiscuity and licentiousness, not in rivalry and jealousy. But put on the Lord Jesus Christ, and make no provision for the desires of the flesh" (Romans 13:13–14). Augustine became a Christian and dedicated himself so totally to his call that he became a great saint and a great theologian who had a great influence on theology for centuries to come.

Paul and Augustine were two men who converted to Christ and became great saints and highly influential theologians in the Church. Their faith in Christ's resurrection led them to dedicate their lives totally to Christ. Their lives teach us that God's grace can touch us (or has already touched us) and bring about miraculous changes in our lives. It is never too late to totally dedicate one's life to Christ.

✠ *What can I learn from this passage?*

Day 3: The Resurrection of the Dead (15:12–34)

Paul and many others who witnessed Christ after his resurrection preach the message that Jesus Christ was raised from the dead. Because of their disregard for the body, the Corinthians had lost sight of the resurrection of the body, but Paul states that faith in resurrection is the basis of their faith in Christ. In this first part of his message, Paul lays the groundwork for what is to follow, namely, to challenge those who claim there is no resurrection.

Paul asks how they can believe that Christ is raised from the dead and yet deny the idea of resurrection from the dead. If there is no resurrection, then they cannot claim Christ has been raised, which means the faith proclaimed by the gospel becomes empty and futile. All those whom Paul named as witnesses in the opening paragraphs of this chapter now become false witnesses and liars. If the Christians at Corinth insist that there is no resurrection from the dead, then they must face the consequences, realize that their faith is useless, and remain in their sins. The belief held by Paul and the apostles was that Jesus overcame the power of evil and brought us to new life through his resurrection. If one does not believe in resurrection from the dead, then those who are deceased no longer exist. Those who place their hopes in Christ only in this life are to be pitied the most, since in misunderstanding faith in their resurrection, they misunderstand the meaning of Christ's death and resurrection.

Paul expresses his own belief by declaring that Jesus is now raised from the dead. He calls him the "firstfruits," a reference to the Old Testament offering that consecrated the harvest to God (Numbers 15:18–21). Through the offering of the firstfruits of the harvest, the Israelites considered their offering to include all the fruits of the harvest. Paul is proclaiming that Christ has consecrated all to God and that all will be raised from the dead because of Christ's resurrection. Paul uses the image of the day when he speaks of those who have fallen asleep in reference to those who have died.

Paul contrasts Christ with Adam, the first human whose sin brought death to creation. Just as Adam sowed the firstfruits of death, so Jesus sowed the firstfruits of life and hope. In Christ, all will be brought to new life, that is, they will be raised to a new life through their resurrection from the dead. Then will come the end of the world, and Jesus will turn over the kingdom to God the Father. The reign of Christ will last until God has placed him over all of his enemies, including death. Paul says that the last enemy to be destroyed will be death, quoting Psalm 8:6 to show that all of Scripture points to the moment when all would be placed under Christ's domain by the Father. All are subject to the Son, who is subject to no one. Jesus willingly subjected himself to the Creator of all when he became human.

The Corinthians apparently had a practice of being baptized on behalf of someone who had already died. We know very little about this practice, since it is mentioned only in this part of the letter to the Corinthians and the practice is found nowhere else in ancient writings. Paul makes no statement about its validity, although he would most likely disagree with it, as shown from the lessons on baptism found in his other letters. He does point to the absurdity of such a practice for those who do not believe in resurrection. If there is no resurrection, how can they carry on the practice of being baptized for the dead?

Paul uses his own suffering as an example of faith in the resurrection. If there were no resurrection, he would be foolish to place himself in so many dangers and hardships. Some Corinthians bragged about their allegiance to Paul, yet without the resurrection, his choice to face death for the gospel would not be praiseworthy but foolish. He alludes to the difficulties he faced in Ephesus, declaring that he certainly profits nothing from such suffering if he accepts it only for human motives. Without resurrection, the pagan attitude toward life ("eat, drink, and be merry, for tomorrow we die") would make sense. Paul urges his readers to stop following those who would lead them astray and to return to the proper way of acting. Because the Corinthian Christians consider knowledge such a great gift, he shames them by calling them ignorant in these matters.

Lectio Divina

Spend 8 to 10 minutes in silent contemplation of the following passage:

Paul, who looked forward to his resurrection in Christ, was willing to suffer all for love of Christ. The driving force for dedicated and saintly Christians is the thought that a joyful resurrection awaits us.

In the last century, there lived a theologian who was truly dedicated to the Lord. He prayed often and believed that all he did was a blessing from the Lord. He loved preaching as much as he loved teaching and writing. Whenever he had an opportunity to preach, he offered special prayers of thanks to the Lord for this privilege.

During his sixty-fifth year of life, the doctors discovered he had cancer of the throat and he underwent an operation that left him with a voice too weak for preaching. When he realized he could no longer preach, he accepted God's will and wrote that the Lord's voice in him was now reduced to a whisper. He received his cross with a smile and continued writing. Years later, when he finally lay on his deathbed, the last words he wrote were, "Now the adventure begins."

Like Paul, this great theologian believed in a joyful resurrection of the dead, and the thought of resurrection motivated him to dedicate his life to Christ. Humanly speaking, many of us may fear and dislike the idea of death, but spiritually speaking, we believe that we will rise to a new and more glorious life in Christ. The resurrection of Jesus becomes our hope for our own resurrection. When we die, the adventure begins.

✠ *What can I learn from this passage?*

Day 4: The Manner of Resurrection (15:35—16)

One of the questions Paul anticipates from his readers concerns the appearance of the body at the time of resurrection. What kind of body will a person have? Paul says the question is a foolish one, thus shaming anyone who would show ignorance by asking it. The seed is planted and must die to produce the plant. The seed is not the body that it is to become, but the seed is a small kernel of wheat or some other plant. God gives whatever body to the seed that God wishes, and each seed produces its own body.

Paul is telling his readers that we give the name "body" to many different categories of life, and everything is not alike. We have human bodies and animal bodies, and even among the animals we have different bodies—those of birds and fish, for example. We have heavenly bodies and earthly bodies, and even the bodies of the heavens—the sun, the moon, the stars—all differ from one another. The stars also differ from one another in brightness. When we apply this use of the term *body* to the resurrection from the dead, we must realize that we are talking about a type of body that differs from the one we now possess. What is sown in the human body is perishable, dishonorable, and weak, and what rises is incorruptible, glorious, and strong. The natural human body dies, and the spiritual body arises. Because we live in a world that does not understand the full meaning of the spiritual body, it is foolish to ask what kind of body we will have at the resurrection.

Paul declares that our natural body necessarily includes our spiritual body, an idea commonly accepted in Greek thought. He speaks of the first Adam, whom we find in the Book of Genesis, as the one who became a living being, and Jesus, the last Adam, as a life-giving spirit. The difference between the two is that the first Adam lived his own life, whereas the second Adam gave life to others through his resurrection. The first Adam belonged to the world, while the second Adam came from above. Just as we, in our human bodies, live in the image of the first Adam, so in our spiritual bodies, we shall live in the image of the second Adam.

Paul wishes to teach that our human condition, the flesh and blood, cannot inherit eternal life because it is not able to merit such a gift. Neither can the corruptible inherit eternal life. A gift of God given through Christ enables a person to enter this incorruptible eternal life. At the end of time, not all will have died, but in an instant, the dead as well as the living will be changed. It will take place in the blink of an eye, at the sound of the last trumpet. The idea of the trumpet call comes from a common image in apocalyptic writing used to announce the end of the world. At the sound of the trumpet, the dead will be raised with an incorruptible body, and the living will be changed, because only the incorruptible and immortal can inherit eternal life. Paul quotes from Hosea (13:14) to declare that the power of death will be defeated. The great weapon of (spiritual) death is sin, and sin gets its power from the law. The victory of Christ will swallow up death, which in Christ has lost its sting and can no longer claim victory. He views the law that has given way to the law of Jesus Christ as losing its power. Paul thanks God for bringing about this victory through the Lord Jesus Christ. He believes the victory comes through the death and resurrection of Christ. He urges the Corinthians to remain steadfast, totally devoted to the work of the Lord with the knowledge that they are not working in vain.

Paul concludes his letter with his plans concerning a visit to Jerusalem with a collection for the Jerusalem church, his travel plans for the future, and greetings from the other churches. The collection was taken up for the church at Jerusalem, which was in need of financial support. The collection would be a visible sign of the unity of the church of God at Corinth with the church of God at Jerusalem. To save time, Paul urges the Corinthians to take up the collection before he arrives, and he promises to send letters of introduction with those who take the collection to Jerusalem. Lest anyone accuse him of using the collection for his own needs, he says he is willing to go to Jerusalem with the collection, but he wants some representatives from the Corinthian community to accompany him.

Paul tells the Corinthian Christians that he will visit with them after he has passed through Macedonia, and he wishes to spend the winter with them, trusting that they will provide for the remainder of his journey, which is most likely directed toward Jerusalem. He states he is presently at Ephesus, where he has found openness to the faith despite some opposition. He urges the members of the Corinthian community to receive Timothy in a gracious manner. Paul is possibly afraid that the Corinthians, so preoccupied with their prestigious position, would reject the apparently insignificant Timothy. He urges them to receive Timothy well and send him on peacefully to meet with Paul. Lest anyone think that Apollos did not visit with them because of some prohibition from him, Paul tells them that he urged Apollos to visit with them, but that Apollos decided on his own to go to them at a more favorable time.

Paul encourages the Corinthians to remain strong in the faith and to continue to live in love. He further urges them to follow the leadership of men like Stephanas, mentioned earlier in this letter as the one who, along with his household, was baptized by Paul (1:16). Stephanas, Fortunatus, and Achaicus had visited Paul, possibly bearing a letter from the Corinthians that is lost to history. Paul urges the community to look to the leadership of these three men for the same nourishment they brought to him. He also sends greetings from the churches of Asia, thus showing his awareness of the Church as universal and adds greetings from Aquila and Prisca, two friends of Paul at Corinth mentioned in the Acts of the Apostles (18:1ff). Aquila and Prisca were apparently living at Ephesus at the time of the writing of the letter. These and all other Christians send their greetings to the Corinthians.

Following a custom of the day, Paul uses his own handwriting for the last few lines of the letter. Ordinarily, a secretary would write the letter as it was dictated, and the speaker would then scribble the last few lines in his own handwriting. This attested to the authenticity of the letter. He curses those who refuse to love the Lord, and he ends with a liturgical prayer that was commonly prayed for the Second Coming of Christ. He wishes them the blessings of Christ and sends his love to all in the name of Christ.

Lectio Divina

Spend 8 to 10 minutes in silent contemplation of the following passage:

Paul anticipates a question people are still asking today, namely, "What kind of body will we have in heaven?" He points out that our new body will be a spiritual body, which means we do not know what it will be. It is pointless to attempt to identify how we will look in heaven. What we look like will most likely not matter as much as the fact that heaven is a state of perfect happiness where we will be sharing in the glorious vision of God. Because we believe in a loving God, we trust that God has a reward prepared for us that is far beyond any beauty we may experience in this life.

A pediatrician ineffectively urged a couple to abort their child, since the child would certainly be born with a number of physical and mental defects and would be a burden to them throughout its life. The baby girl, named Patricia, was born with the predicted defects, but the child grew into adulthood as a smiling and happy human being who was able to bring joy into the lives of many others. Her parents would wheel her out onto the porch where people in the neighborhood would come and enjoy a visit with her.

Patricia touched the hearts of so many people that when she died at the age of forty, people in the neighborhood asked, "What is life going to be without Patricia sitting on her porch?" Some added, "I'll bet she is the prettiest woman in heaven," and, "Her smile and courage made my problems seem so small."

What will we look like in heaven? Who cares? All we can say is that Patricia will be beautiful, whatever that means. Heaven is the total fulfillment of love, a love so powerful that we can never imagine the attainment of such love in this life. Whatever God has in store for those who remain faithful will be an astounding experience of love fulfilled. According to Paul, those who remain devoted to the Lord to the end will discover that their labors were not in vain.

✠ *What can I learn from this passage?*

Review Questions

1. What do you think of the ritual established by Paul for using the gifts of the Holy Spirit?

2. Why was it important for Paul to establish his call as an apostle?

3. What reasons does Paul give for believing in the resurrection of the dead?

4. What is Paul's image of the role of Christ in God's total plan of creation?

5. How does Paul's image of resurrection compare with your thoughts about resurrection?

Ministers of the New Covenant

2 CORINTHIANS 1—5

For we know that if our earthly dwelling, a tent, should be destroyed, we have a building from God, a dwelling not made with hands, eternal in heaven (5:1).

Opening Prayer (SEE PAGE 18)

Context

Part 1: 2 Corinthians 1—3:6 In Paul's Second Letter to the Corinthians, he reveals a variety of moods and emotions. The letter gives us an image of Paul as a man who is angry, compassionate, forgiving, loving, and sorrowful. Many commentators believe the letter is actually a collection of excerpts from several letters written by Paul. Although these various collections express Paul's different emotions and reactions to some situations existing within Corinth, they are all similar in a style and attitude that reflect Paul's personality. They were not necessarily written in the order found in 2 Corinthians.

When Paul first learned the Corinthians wanted him to visit them, he wrote a *letter of defense concerning his ministry*. Commentators believe this letter is contained in chapters 2:14—7:2, with the exception of 6:14—7:1, which is a disputed passage. Paul sent this letter to Corinth with Titus, who upon his return to Paul, reported that some problems had arisen at Corinth. Paul then visited Corinth himself, but his visit was an apparent failure. After Paul's visit to Corinth, he wrote *a letter of tears* (chapters 10—13). Titus took this letter to the Corinthians. When he later met Paul at Macedonia, he told him how well the Corinthians had received his letter. Happy with this news, Paul then wrote a *letter of reconciliation* (chapters 1:1—2:13 and 7:5-16).

In his *letter of reconciliation*, Paul greets the Corinthians and introduces himself as an apostle of Jesus Christ, revealing that he willingly suffers affliction to encourage them to remain faithful. He defends his sincere desire to visit with the Corinthians and explains why he was not able to visit them as promised. He says his promise is as sincere as that of Jesus Christ, but he did not come to them since he would have inflicted pain upon them with his exhortations. He then urges them to accept back into the community someone he ordered them to expel in his first letter, since the person has repented.

Part 2: 2 Corinthians 3:7—5 Paul offers himself as an oblation for the Lord. So that the members of the church at Corinth do not misunderstand him, he states that he does not boast of himself but of them and their dedication to the Lord. He makes a reference to Moses and his need to cover his face after receiving the commandments, and he states that the reason for the veil was to hide the idea that the Old Covenant was gradually fading. With the New Covenant, the veil is removed and people are able to gaze on the glory of the Lord freely. The new has surpassed the old to such a degree that the glory of the new makes the glory of the old disappear. He views the new as still veiled for those who are perishing. Despite his afflictions and suffering, Paul declares that he has given himself up for the Lord, and this frees him from all discouragement. Paul compares his life on earth to a tent that may be destroyed, but he has faith in an eternal home given by God. This faith leads to courage. Because of his attachment to the Lord, Paul will no longer view others in the flesh but as a new creation in Christ.

PART 1: GROUP STUDY (2 CORINTHIANS 1—3:6)

Read aloud 2 Corinthians 1—3:6.

1:1–11 Greeting and thanksgiving

Paul begins his letter to the Corinthians with a simple but common formula used by the Greeks. He first identifies himself as the sender and Timothy as his companion. Then he addresses a special greeting to those to whom the letter is sent. Although Paul does not identify himself as an apostle of Christ Jesus in all his letters, he must have felt a special need to use this title as he wrote to the Corinthians, who placed a high value on such authority. The tone of the letter clearly reveals the reason Paul feels a need to underline his authority for this particular audience. As an apostle, Paul speaks the message of Jesus, not by his own choice, but by the will of God. Paul was always conscious of his special call by God on the road to Damascus, which brought him to faith in Christ (Acts 9:1–30).

Timothy, also mentioned in the greeting, is Paul's companion at the time the letter was written. Timothy was a Christian from Lystra in Asia Minor who joined Paul in his missionary work. He was already known to the people of Corinth and recognized as a beloved friend and ambassador for Paul to the church of Corinth. As he did in his First Letter to the Corinthians, Paul addresses the letter to "the church of God that is in Corinth," signifying the unity of the church at Corinth with the universal Church. Corinth was in the province of Achaia, so Paul addresses his readers as the holy ones throughout Achaia. When Paul addresses his readers as "the holy ones," he is addressing them as people who have accepted baptism in the name of Christ. In his greeting, Paul links the Greek greeting ("grace") with the Hebrew greeting ("peace"), thus signifying that the church at Corinth has elements of Greek and Hebrew backgrounds. As an apostle, Paul offers this grace and peace in the name of God the Father and the Lord Jesus Christ.

The normal procedure in ancient writings was to follow a greeting with some form of thanksgiving. Paul uses his words of praise as a spontaneous thanksgiving to God for the gifts he has received. The reason for praise and thanksgiving to God is threefold: God is the Father of Christ, God is

merciful, and God is compassionate. Just as God offers comfort in affliction, so God allows the apostle to offer this same comfort to others. Not
only does the apostle share in the sufferings of Jesus Christ but also in the
comfort of Jesus Christ. The sufferings of Paul, as well as the consolation
given, are offered to the Corinthians as encouragement to accept their
own sufferings. Paul recognizes the suffering being endured by many in
the Corinthian community, and he hopes to offer them encouragement
as they recall Christ's suffering and consolation (as well as his own) as a
hope for consolation in the midst of their despair.

Paul then speaks of a difficulty he faced while in Asia, although he does
not name the particular event. He had many occasions for suffering in Asia,
and the one to which he refers had been so terrible that it threatened to
lead to his death. At this moment of greatest weakness, Paul declares that
his only hope was in God's power to raise the dead to life. God rescued
him and his companions from this brush with death, and he has confi-
dent hope that God will continue to do so. In his efforts to praise God in
thanksgiving, Paul asks the Corinthians to help him with their prayers.
Paul expresses his belief that the gifts from God have come as a result of
the prayers of many.

1:12–22 Paul's total dedication

Paul has already visited with the Corinthians, and they know of his honesty
and sincerity. He tells his readers that his conscience witnesses to what he
tells them as well as to his manner of acting among them. His call comes
not from his own worldly wisdom but from God. Because of the source
of this call, Paul acts as one who shares the Word of God with holiness
and openness, and he shares the message in a way that they can read and
comprehend. In this way, Paul contrasts himself with the wise writers of
the day who were difficult to understand and who were more interested
in portraying their ability to speak profoundly than in presenting their
message. He identifies himself as the one about whom the Corinthians can
boast, just as they are the ones he can boast about on the day of the Lord's
Second Coming. Their boast is not about themselves but about what they
find in Paul. In the same way, Paul's boast is not about himself but about
the faithful response the Christians at Corinth are giving to his message.

Paul considers his visits to the people of Corinth to be a blessing, since he comes as an apostle of Jesus Christ. He apparently planned to visit the Corinthians twice—first on his way to Macedonia, and second on his return journey to Judea. He mentions that he wanted to seek their help on his way to Judea. This may be a reference to the support they would offer him by way of encouragement, or it may refer to financial support for the suffering Christians of Judea. Although Paul had expressed these plans earlier with a promise to visit the Corinthians, he was unable to fulfill his promise.

Paul was accused by some members of the Corinthian church of being insincere when he promised to visit them, while others seemed to claim that Paul was fickle in making promises, easily changing his mind when the need arose. These accusations most likely hurt Paul deeply, since they came from the church he himself had founded and from people he loved. Paul may have viewed these accusations as a threat to the Corinthians' faith in his message about Christ. As an apostle, Paul declares that he keeps his word, just as God does in fulfilling the promises made throughout the Scriptures. Like God, Paul does not need to swear under oath, but as a true apostle chosen by God through Christ, his "yes" should be as acceptable as that of Jesus Christ. He reminds the Corinthians that he preached about Jesus as the Son of God, and he recalls that Jesus' life was a continual "yes." As a witness to his message about Jesus, Paul reminds the Corinthians that he was accompanied by Silvanus and Timothy, who preached this message with him. Paul states that his life is a continual "yes" to God, just as Jesus' life was a continual "yes." God's sincerity was proved through the promises that were fulfilled in Christ. Because of this candor of God in the fulfillment of the promises, Paul declares that we can call out our "Amen" as we worship God through Christ.

Paul reminds the Corinthians that it is from God, the one who fulfills promises, that he has received his call. He uses the baptismal images of anointing, sealing, and giving the Spirit. Through baptism, Paul has become fully one with Christ and one with all Christians, including the Christians of Corinth. Through his call, Paul recognizes that he must imitate Christ and declare that he does not act with fickleness or insincerity.

1:23—2:13 Reason for Paul's change of plans

Although Paul founded the church at Corinth, he had no desire to dominate the Christians in Corinth. He had apparently received some news at the time that would have led to his chastening the people. Rather than dampen their happiness and joy, Paul chose not to visit with them at that time. Because he did not want to make his visit a painful one, he decided to send them a letter instead. The letter he sent has been labeled the *letter of tears* by some commentators. Since 2 Corinthians is apparently a collection of several letters sent by Paul, commentators suggest that his *letter of tears* is found in chapters 10 to 13 of this letter, while others consider the reproachful tone of 1 Corinthians to be the *letter of tears* written by Paul.

Paul realized he would have no choice but to chastise those bringing harm to the community, and this chastisement would cause him great pain. The only ones who could relieve him of that pain would be the ones he chastised. Trusting that they were concerned as much for his happiness as he was for theirs, Paul wrote to them in anguish and with many tears. His letter was not intended to cause them pain, but to call them to a change of heart. The letter, though harsh, was written as an expression of Paul's love for the Corinthians.

Paul writes about someone in the community who has apparently caused pain by acting against the message he preached. Paul reminds the community that such a person has sinned not only against him, but also against the community. The offense and the offender are unknown to us. Whoever the offender is, the person apparently has received ample punishment and repented, and Paul now urges the community to forgive him or her so that the person's sorrow does not become overwhelming. The purpose of punishment is not to crush the offender, but to lead the person to repentance. Paul encourages the community to receive this person with love. He admits he had written to the community urging them to punish the offenders in their midst, but he now calls on them to extend forgiveness to those amply punished. If the community decides to forgive the offender, Paul declares he will do the same. He willingly forgives for the sake of Christ that the offender may not feel abandoned by the Christian community and thus be led to further temptation and sin. Paul views Satan as ready to take advantage of the situation.

When Paul went on to Troas, he found a good opportunity for preaching the gospel, but he felt anxiety at not finding Titus at Troas. Titus was a companion as close to him as Timothy. Titus would have news for Paul concerning the people of Corinth, and Paul was anxious to hear that news. Paul goes on to Macedonia in search of Titus.

2:14—3:6 Ministers of a new covenant

Because of the abrupt change in Paul's message found in 2:14, many commentators agree that this passage signifies the beginning of another letter by Paul, added at this point by a later editor. It is possible that Paul himself gathered the letters together into one letter. The passage shifts from Paul's concern for Titus to a spontaneous expression of thanksgiving to God. The thanksgiving formula follows the opening greeting in ancient Greek letters. Since the greeting is already contained at the beginning of the first letter, the editor could have chosen to begin with the thanksgiving prayer. Other commentators claim the section tells of Paul's relief and joy at finding Titus and hearing that the Corinthians received him well. Paul's prayer of thanksgiving then becomes a prayer of praise for the goodness shown by God.

Paul uses a common victory image of his day as he speaks of being part of Christ's triumphal procession. In ancient times, a victorious leader would march with his army and prisoners in a triumphant parade that extolled the extent of his conquests. Paul thanks God that he belongs to this triumphal procession of Christ, although he does not state whether he sees himself as one of the soldiers or as a slave. In his writings, Paul more often sees himself as a servant of the Lord.

Paul pictures himself as the aroma of Christ that reaches in praise to God the Father. In the Hebrew sacrifice, an animal would be killed and parts of the animal, or the whole animal, would be burned as a pleasing fragrance to the Lord. In the Book of Leviticus, we read that Aaron's sons shall burn the offering on the altar "as a sweet-smelling oblation to the LORD" (3:5). For those who believe in Christ, the fragrance of one's offering of self will bring salvation, but it will bring destruction to unbelievers.

Paul recognizes that no one is truly worthy of this mission to bring Christ to the nations, yet he proclaims he is doing it, not for the sake of any personal reward, but for the sake of Christ. In doing this, he differs from some preachers of his day who have made their preaching of the Word of God a source of income. Paul declares he is aware of God's call in his life, and he is conscious of living continuously in God's presence.

Paul continues to answer objections from the Corinthian community. Although we do not have any record of these objections, we can catch a hint of some of them from the manner in which Paul writes his letter. He feels a need to respond to two objections at this point. First, some have apparently accused Paul of boasting; second, some have accused him of traveling without the customary letters of recommendation from some other Church authorities. Paul answers the second objection first.

Paul recognizes that he does not have such a letter of recommendation, but he tells the Corinthians that they are his living letter, known to others not because of some message written in ink, but because of a message written in their hearts. Paul recalls the stone tablets given by God to Moses (Exodus 24:12), and he states that his letter of recommendation is not written on stone tablets but on tablets of the human heart. An Old Testament prophet, Jeremiah, spoke of God's writing the law on the hearts of the Israelites (31:33). The authority for Paul's letter of recommendation is not some important figure of the early Church, but it is the Spirit of God, who alone can write on the hearts of the people.

Although Paul could appear to speak foolishly to those who have no faith, he proclaims he speaks in this manner because of his trust in God through Christ. He states he can take no credit for himself, since God has qualified him and his companions as ministers of the new covenant. The new covenant is not a written law, but a law of the Spirit. Unlike the written law of Moses, which simply pointed out sin and could not give life, the law of the Spirit gives life.

Review Questions

1. What experiences gave Paul the ability to offer encouragement to the church at Corinth?

2. Paul hesitates to go to the Corinthians when they were offending God. What does this tell us about his personality?

3. Using the image of his own life as a sweet aroma to God, Paul reveals his attitude toward the New Covenant. Explain and share with your group Paul's understanding as found in this passage of Scripture.

4. What did Paul mean when he said that the Corinthians were his letter of recommendation? What does he mean when he says that the veil is lifted in the New Testament?

Closing Prayer (SEE PAGE 18)

Pray the closing prayer now or after *lectio divina*.

Lectio Divina (SEE PAGE 11)

Relax your body and maintain a posture of prayer (back straight, eyes shut, feet flat on the floor). This exercise can take as long as you want, but in the context of this Bible study, 10 to 20 minutes should be sufficient.

The meditations that follow are provided only to help group participants use this prayer form, but note that *lectio* is intended to bring one to a place of prayerful contemplation where the Word of God speaks to the hearer from his or her heart. (See page 11 for further instruction.)

Greeting and thanksgiving (1:1–11)

When Paul speaks of himself as suffering for the salvation of the Corinthians, he is following an attitude about suffering found in the prophets of the Old Testament and in the life of Jesus. In the Book of Isaiah, the prophet speaks of a suffering servant, saying he was crushed with pain, making his life "a reparation offering" (53:10). Isaiah was introducing the idea that a person could suffer in reparation for the sins of others. At the Last Supper, Jesus blessed the wine and said that this "is my blood of the covenant, which will be shed on behalf of many for the forgiveness of sins" (Matthew 26:28).

According to Christian teaching, suffering has value when offered in union with the suffering of Jesus. In a rural hospital, a saintly man whose whole body was wracked with pain from arthritis offered his suffering for peace in the world. Each movement made him wince in pain. He believed that when his pain became more intense, his suffering became a greater form of prayer for someone in special need of help. He was grateful that God allowed suffering to be a powerful prayer for others.

Paul says to the Christians at Corinth, "If we are afflicted, it is for your encouragement and salvation" (1:6). Paul not only offers his suffering as a prayer, but he offers it as an example for others to follow. Jesus' suffering was not just something that happened to him in life; it was a means of bringing salvation to the world. Although Christians should work to alleviate all suffering, the Scriptures teach us that unavoidable suffering can be a powerful form of prayer.

✠ *What can I learn from this passage?*

Paul's total dedication (1:12–22)

In the Gospel of Matthew (5:37), we read that Jesus told his listeners not to use oaths but to be so totally honest that people would accept their word without an oath. He said they should make their "yes" mean "yes" and their "no" mean "no." Although the Gospel of Matthew was not yet in its final form when Paul wrote this letter to the Corinthians, Paul may have been referring to this teaching of Jesus that was being preached long before the final editor of the gospel wrote these words. Paul says his "yes," like that of Christ, is "yes," meaning he was a dedicated, good, and truthful person.

In a story about Thomas More, King Henry VIII is trying to convince Thomas to sign a declaration stating that the ruler of England was the head of the Church in England. When Thomas asked Henry why it was so important for him to have Thomas sign the declaration, the king responded that everyone knew Thomas was a good man, faithful to his word, and to God. If Thomas signed the declaration, then others would agree to do the same. Thomas, as history tells us, accepted death rather than turn against the Pope as the head of the Church. Thomas was a man whose "yes" was "yes" and whose "no" was "no."

This is what Paul would wish for all of us in calling us to follow his example and that of Christ in making our "yes" a "yes" and our "no" a "no." We would all like to be identified as a good, dedicated, and truthful person.

✠ *What can I learn from this passage?*

Reason for Paul's change of plans (1:23—2:13)

When Paul converted to Christ, the Church members who knew of Paul's persecution of the followers of Christ hesitated to accept him into the community, believing Paul's apparent conversion was a trick used by him to infiltrate and further persecute the Church. A man named Joseph received the name Barnabas from the community because he was a faithful and trusting follower of Christ. The name Barnabas means "son of encouragement." It was Barnabas who accepted Paul as an authentic follower of Christ.

When Paul speaks in this passage of welcoming sinners back into the community when they repent, he may have learned much about forgiveness from his own experience with Barnabas. Without someone like Barnabas, Paul may not have become the great apostle he became. God sent a son of encouragement to Paul, and as strange as it may sound, Paul needed someone like Barnabas to begin his mission. Barnabas's example illustrates for all of us how to be forgiving and encouraging people. He teaches us that Christianity is meant to be a joyful and encouraging faith, dedicated to trusting Jesus as a companion in life.

✠ *What can I learn from this passage?*

Ministers of a new covenant (2:14—3:6)

Jesus tells a parable about a servant who works all day plowing or tending sheep. When the servant comes in from the field, his master does not tell him to take a place at table so the master can wait on him. Instead, he tells his servant to wait on him while he eats. Jesus tells us that his followers are those servants who say, "We are unprofitable servants; we have done what we were obliged to do" (Luke 17:10).

Paul views himself as an unprofitable servant, doing what he is obliged to do for the Lord. He does not commend himself, but he points to others as his letter of recommendation as a servant of the Lord. The Lord will look to the Corinthians to determine whether his servant Paul has served well.

Like a true servant, Paul has worked at sharing the faith with the Christians in Corinth. Although he has done well, the Lord owes him nothing in return, and when the Lord rewards him with eternal life, it is still a gift. In the same way, the Lord will look to those we serve in our life and determine whether they will be a living letter of recommendation for God to grant us the gift of eternal life.

✠ *What can I learn from this passage?*

PART 2: INDIVIDUAL STUDY (2 CORINTHIANS 3:7—5)

Day 1: Contrast With the Old Covenant (3:7–18)

When Moses received the law, his face shone brightly due to his encounter with God. The writer of Exodus describes how Moses had to cover his face with a veil because the glory of God reflected through Moses' countenance (34:27–35). Paul refers to this event when he speaks of the great glory of the new law. If the glory of God shone so brightly in the giving of the old law, how much more brightly will God's glory shine through the ministry of the Spirit in the giving of the new law?

For Paul, the law of Moses identified sin for people, and in doing this, it became a condemning law. The new law, however, brings justification, which brings with it more glory. Paul declares such glory to be so great that the glory of the old disappears when compared with the glory of the new. The old law was meant to give way to the new law, which comes through the Spirit. If this is so, then the glory of the old law, which is meant to pass away, becomes a witness to the greater glory of the new law, which is not meant to pass away.

In light of the glory of the new law, Paul lives with complete trust in God. Although the Exodus story tells us that Moses wore the veil because the people could not look at his face and live, Paul offers a different interpretation. Paul declares that Moses hid his face so that the people of Israel could not see the fading glory of the old law. Paul adds that even during his era, some do not see the fading of the old law, and when they listen to the message of the Scriptures, it is veiled to them so that they are not able to understand. They do not understand that the old glory has given way to a new glory. Only through faith in Christ will the veil be removed.

Paul refers to the Spirit as "Lord" in this passage, an implication that the Spirit is also Lord along with the Father and the Son. In this Spirit, Christians find freedom, and they can look on the glory of the Lord with unveiled faces. Just as Moses grew in glory through his encounters with the Lord, Christians continue to grow in glory in this same way. They are gradually being transformed into the image of the Lord, whom Paul again calls "the Spirit."

Lectio Divina

Spend 8 to 10 minutes in silent contemplation of the following passage:

Paul teaches that those who adhere stubbornly to the law of Moses and refuse to accept Christ view God's plan only dimly. The real glory of God's creation is Jesus Christ. Even those of us who believe that Jesus is the Christ must meditate daily on the mysteries of God become human in Jesus Christ. Our faith deepens gradually as we continue to contemplate God's great love in our life.

In the Gospel of Mark (8:22–26), we read of a blind man healed by Jesus. At first, the blind man could only see dimly. He saw people as if they were walking trees. When Jesus touched him again, he saw clearly and realized that the people were distinct from the trees.

Paul uses the same type of image when speaking of the people who lived by the law of Moses. Throughout the Old Testament, they were meant to see only part of God's plan for creation. When Jesus came as the Christ, they were meant to see more clearly. People received the call not only to live the law, but to live in the Spirit of Christ, which was a spirit of love of God, neighbor, and self.

The Spirit lifts the veil, and those who believe in Christ clearly understand God's plan of creation. Just as Christ had to move the blind man gradually from blindness to seeing dimly to seeing clearly, so God's revelation comes to us gradually. In the Spirit, the old gives way to the new.

✠ *What can I learn from this passage?*

Day 2: Ministry to the Message of Jesus (4:1–18)

Because Paul has no desire for earthly gain from his ministry, and he has no doubt that he has been called to it by God, he remains firm, not allowing himself to become discouraged. Some of his opponents have apparently accused Paul of using underhanded and cunning methods in his ministry. He declares that he rejects such methods and preaches with candor, openly sharing the truth with all people and willing to stand before God in the judgment of all concerning his ministry.

Some have apparently accused Paul of preaching the gospel in images that are hard to understand, but he claims the message is veiled only for those intent on destruction. The desire for material goods and the lure of the world have dulled their minds to the message he preaches. The light of Christ cannot shine in the inner darkness of those who choose the world as their god. Paul declares that he does not preach about himself but about Jesus Christ, who is the Lord. He sees his own mission as that of a servant to the people of Corinth for the sake of Jesus. Quoting from the Book of Genesis (1:3), Paul reminds the Corinthians that God said, "Let light shine out of darkness." He applies this light to the inner light leading to an understanding and a sharing of the message of God as shown through Jesus Christ.

Paul uses the image of clay jars to show that God chooses apostles as fragile as clay vessels to preach the gospel. Because of their weakness, the apostles cannot claim any strength in themselves but must admit that all power and strength come from God. With faith in God's power, the apostles undergo every type of persecution and affliction without despairing or losing heart. This persecution has a value for Paul; it points to the apostles' unity with the suffering and death of Jesus. Instead of leading to eternal death, the suffering of the apostles leads to life in Jesus. Paul uses the name "Jesus" in this passage instead of "Jesus Christ" to emphasize that he is speaking of the suffering endured by Jesus during his earthly life. The title "Christ" expresses recognition that Jesus is the one who conquered sin and death through his resurrection from the dead. Here Paul is speaking about Jesus before his resurrection.

The ministry of the apostles, according to Paul, is not only for preaching, but it requires suffering in union with Jesus. He stresses that this suffering may lead to a physical death, but it brings eternal life to the Corinthians. Quoting from Psalm 116:10, Paul states that the logical outcome of faith is sharing God's message. Because of their faith, the apostles preach the gospel with the hope of sharing in the resurrection of Jesus, as do the Corinthians. The larger the number of Corinthians who turn to God in faith, the greater the praise and thanksgiving given to God.

Paul offers encouragement to his listeners as he makes a distinction between the sufferings encountered in his earthly body and the reward that awaits those who serve God. His earthly body is wasting away, as all earthly bodies do, but this does not discourage Paul, who keeps his vision on an eternal reward. Paul lives with faith, looking toward that which is unseen (an eternal glory beyond all imagination) and not toward that which passes away (the material necessities of life).

Lectio Divina

Spend 8 to 10 minutes in silent contemplation of the following passage:

Paul received the call to believe in Christ and to share his message, as Christians do, but the call does not change a person from a fragile earthen vessel into a superperson. God has called all believers from among the human family. In reality, this is the strength of being a Christian. It means living in this world with all our human weaknesses, with fear, doubts, insecurity, and a countless number of temptations.

The greatest manifestation of God's love for us occurred when "the Word became flesh and made his dwelling among us" (John 1:14). According to Luke's Gospel, the Word of God became a child who was born in poverty and rejected by his own people. As we read about the life of Jesus throughout the gospels, we learn that he became hungry, thirsty, tired, frustrated, angry, and that he could suffer pain, as he did in his passion. Jesus came among us as a fragile human being, like us in every way except sin. He became as fragile as an earthen vessel.

The value of being faithful to Christ comes from the reality that we are weak, fragile human beings attempting to remain faithful through life. If God helped us to rise above this fragile human existence as ministers of Christ, we would no longer be a powerful gift to God. It is in weakness, as earthen vessels, that our life can become a gift to God, just as God gave us a gift in becoming human.

✠ *What can I learn from this passage?*

Day 3: Living by Faith, Not by Sight (5:1–10)

Paul uses an image familiar to the people of his day. During their long journeys through the desert, travelers relied on their tents as a place of protection against the elements. When the traveler was ready to move on, the tent would be folded up and carried. The image of folding up one's life like a tent was used in the Old Testament as an image of death. In the Book of Isaiah we read, "My dwelling, like a shepherd's tent, is struck down and borne away from me; You have folded up my life, like a weaver who severs me from the last thread" (38:12). Paul is telling his readers that our earthly tent (our bodies) will be folded up in death but that the eternal dwelling place—made by God and not by any human tentmaker—will provide a new covering for a person who reaches eternal life.

Because heaven is our true dwelling place, we groan while we are here, longing for the heavenly dwelling to completely envelop us. Paul uses the imagery of this heavenly dwelling to symbolize some type of clothing that keeps us from appearing naked. To the ancient Hebrews, nakedness was considered a form of deep humiliation and shame. As one sheds this earthly dwelling place, a new covering comes in the form of the heavenly one and completely envelops the one who is faithful. This dwelling does more than clothe us; it also absorbs us who are mortal into a state of immortality, which Paul calls "life." This call to an eternal dwelling place comes from God, and as a guarantee of this call to life, God has given us the Spirit.

Because of this pledge that comes from the presence of the Spirit, Paul can proclaim his confidence in the Lord. As long as a person lives in the body, he or she is living away from the Lord, who is spiritual. Life in the body is a life of faith, since a person is not able to see with human eyes the fulfillment of his or her call. Although Paul would rather be freed from the body to be with the Lord, he is willing to follow God's will, whether that will calls Paul to continue in his earthly body or calls him to eternal glory. Paul mentions the judgment, reminding his readers that each one will receive a reward according to the manner of one's life, the manner in which a person truly lives in this earthly dwelling.

Lectio Divina

Spend 8 to 10 minutes in silent contemplation of the following passage:

Paul did not always depend on those he converted to Christ to provide for his needs. He was a tentmaker who sold tents to support himself. As a tentmaker, he would naturally think of a tent as he preached his message.

An elderly man who often used Paul's image of a tent in his meditations throughout his life told a faith-sharing group that when he was a youth, he saw his body as a new and shiny tent. As he grew older, the material of the tent became more hardened from the rain and cold. His life, like a tent, had to endure every bit of sunshine and rain, the good days and bad days. When he grew to old age, as he was when he was sharing his thoughts, he saw his body as a worn-out tent, sagging in the middle, allowing some of the rain and cold to slip in, spoiling his warmth and rest. He looked forward to the day when he could finally fold up the tent that was his body and bring its tattered rags to God, who would replace it with a resplendent new dwelling place in eternal glory.

As Christians, we believe that when our bodies are folded up like a tent, we are not left naked in our worldly hopes, but we enter a new life, clothed in the Spirit. For a Christian, death means going home to the Lord. Paul longs to go home to the Lord, but he has a mission to accomplish. We, too, have a mission. As long as we are on this earth, whatever field of work we pursue, whatever our age, whatever joys or difficulties we encounter, whatever is the condition of our tent, we have our mission until the day God calls us. If we live well, close to God, we finally fold up our tent and go home to the Lord.

✠ *What can I learn from this passage?*

Day 4: Ministry of Reconciliation (5:11–21)

Paul continues to defend himself against his attackers. He tells the Corinthians that his reverential fear of the Lord leads him in his quest to spread the gospel. His motives are known to God and (he hopes) to the people of the Corinthian community. Paul has commended himself to the Corinthians in previous writings, and he promises not to do so again in this letter. He challenges them to choose what they wish from his activities and to boast about them to others who place such a high regard on external appearances as opposed to internal integrity. If the Corinthians had previously thought of Paul's activities as strange in some way, Paul now tells them to recognize his activities as done in service of God. When Paul acts in a way that wins human approval, he does so not for himself, but for the Corinthians. Paul's actions have their source in his love for Christ, and he believes that Christ's death brought all to a new life in Christ. This life should lead them to live for Christ rather than for themselves. The source of Paul's own foolishness is the death and resurrection of Christ, which brings a new life and meaning to creation.

Before his conversion to Christ, Paul saw the world through human eyes alone, and he saw Christ as a mere human being. His viewpoint changed, however, after his conversion. Now he sees the world as a new creation in union with Christ. The old way has been overcome by the new. God has reconciled the world through Christ, and this reconciliation is being brought to the world by Christ's followers. The apostle is the minister of this reconciliation, the one through whom God appeals to all people to accept such a reconciliation. Paul begs the Corinthians to accept it. For all of us, God made Christ, who was sinless, to be sin. Paul does not see Christ as a sinner but as the one who carries on his shoulders the effects of sin for the sake of reconciliation. Through his reconciliation, offered by God, we share in the depth of God's holiness.

Lectio Divina

Spend 8 to 10 minutes in silent contemplation of the following passage:

Paul says that whoever is in Christ is a new creation, and he calls on the Corinthians to reconcile themselves with God. Christians believe that we actually become a new creation through our baptism, but the challenge is to live up to the truth that we have clothed ourselves in Christ and now live in Christ.

Father Tim returned to a parish he had served ten years earlier for the fiftieth anniversary of the current pastor. During the celebration of the Eucharist, he noticed a man in the assembly who more than ten years earlier had confronted him about his (Father Tim's) belief in Christ. The man was baptized Catholic as a child, but as a teenager, he believed that faith in Jesus was a false tale used to control people's minds. At the time, the man told Father Tim that he was an atheist, and he added that he could not understand how a man as intelligent as Father Tim could believe in Christ.

Later, at the reception following the celebration of the Eucharist, Father Tim pulled aside one of the women in the parish whom he knew well and asked about the atheist who had confronted him years earlier. The parishioner told him that the man who once claimed to be an atheist did a great deal of reading and eventually came to believe in God. Not only did he convert to Christ, but he now participated in daily Eucharist, helped with almost every function in the parish, and taught religious education. Father Tim shook his head with a smile and said, "Now here's a good example of someone putting on Christ. He looks the same, but he is definitely a different person."

Christianity is not only a matter of knowing about Jesus, but one of knowing Jesus. It means we are baptized into Christ. For many, the challenge of Christianity is living what we already are. The man who claimed to be an atheist was already baptized, but he had to learn to live what he already was. He had to learn to live as a baptized Christian.

✠ *What can I learn from this passage?*

Review Questions

1. Why does Paul believe that the face of Moses was veiled to show the fading glory of the old law?

2. In what ways are we earthen vessels?

3. Why is it so difficult for most people to accept that someday they will fold up the tent of their body and move on to God?

4. How courageous does our faith make us? Reflect on a few examples of courage in your own life.

5. Are we conscious of living as new creations in Christ?

An Acceptable Time

2 CORINTHIANS 6—9

"In an acceptable time I heard you, and on the day of salvation I helped you." Behold, now is a very acceptable time; behold, now is the day of salvation (6:2).

Opening Prayer (SEE PAGE 18)

Context

Part 1: 2 Corinthians 6—7 Paul speaks of his dedication to his ministry, accepting all forms of affliction for the sake of the Lord. He declares that Christians are the temple of God and should have nothing to do with the temple of idols. Titus informs Paul that he has saddened the Corinthian Christians with his letter, but Paul does not regret it, since he believes it will sadden them for only a short period. He rejoices in their repentance.

Part 2: 2 Corinthians 8—9 Paul praises the Corinthian Christians for their generosity, urging them to give generously with the same spirit that they exhibit in practicing so many other virtues. He tells the Corinthians to give with balance, without denying their own needs. Sending brothers ahead to arrange for the generous monetary offering of the Corinthians, Paul reminds his readers that they will reap what they sow. He notes that the day could come when the church at Jerusalem will be called upon to supply the needs of the church at Corinth.

PART 1: GROUP STUDY (2 CORINTHIANS 6—7)

Read aloud 2 Corinthians 6—7.

6:1–13 The acceptable time

Paul warns the Corinthians not to misuse God's gifts. He quotes from Isaiah (49:8), who speaks in the name of God when he proclaims that he has heard the people at an acceptable time and has helped them on the day of salvation. Paul further tells the Corinthians that the present moment is the acceptable time and the day of salvation. The phrase "day of salvation" refers to the new life given through Christ that will reach its fulfillment at the end of time. In sharing the gospel message, Paul avoids giving offense so that the message may not be clouded by his conduct. He would rather present himself as a minister of God with patience and endurance.

Paul follows a custom of his day in listing his trials. He first presents a general list (afflictions, hardships, and calamities); then those sufferings inflicted by others (beatings, imprisonments, riots); and finally those he personally accepted (labors, sleepless nights, and hunger). He acts with purity, knowledge, patience, kindness, genuine love, truthful speech, and the power of God. Paul portrays these virtues as weapons used by a person about to engage in battle. Like a warrior, he holds his weapon in his right hand and his shield in his left. In this passage, Paul notes the contrast between what the followers of Christ are called and what they truly are. They are described as impostors, unknown, dying, sorrowful, and having nothing. In reality, they are true, well known, alive, rejoicing, able to enrich many, and actually possessing everything in life. His offense is his many good deeds, and he defends against false accusations. Paul tells the Corinthians he has opened his heart to them, but they have not done the same for him. He invites them to respond.

6:14—7:4 The temple of the living God

Some commentators have reservations about one small section of the letter that seems to shift too dramatically from the context in which it is found

(6:14—7:1). Paul is speaking in defense of his mission, and he suddenly reminds the people that they are the temple of the living God and that they should act in accordance with this gift. Some commentators claim this section was added to the letter at a later date by another writer, while others claim it is an excerpt from an earlier letter written by Paul. The passage digresses from the theme Paul has been developing in this part of his letter. It contains words not used by Paul, and it fits awkwardly into this section. We can come to no clear decision whether this passage was or was not written by Paul.

Paul writes that just as there is no compatibility between righteousness and lawlessness, light and darkness, Christ and Beliar, so there is no compatibility between believers and unbelievers. The term *Beliar* refers to the devil. Paul reminds the Corinthians that they are the temple of God and that there is no compatibility between the temple of God and the temple of idols. Furthermore, he teaches that the Corinthians are the temple of God by quoting from the Book of Leviticus (26:12) in which the one true God chooses to dwell among the people, making them the people of God. Quoting from Isaiah (52:11), Paul exhorts the people to move away from unbelievers and to touch nothing unclean. By quoting from 2 Samuel (7:14), Paul completes this series of Scripture quotes that remind believers of their inheritance as sons or daughters. Paul uses these quotations to motivate the Corinthians to avoid every human defilement and to faithfully live their dedication to God.

7:5–16 Saddened into repentance

Paul wishes to express his love for the Corinthians, and he reminds them that he has not unjustly hurt anyone in any way. Neither does he condemn them for anything they have done. He has a joyful love for them, despite the many sufferings they have caused him. He tells them how much he boasts about them.

In an earlier passage of this letter (2:13), Paul told of his trip to Macedonia, where he anxiously looked for his companion Titus, whom he had sent on to Corinth. His anxiety ends at Macedonia, where he meets Titus and receives good news concerning the people of Corinth. Paul had apparently written an earlier letter (his letter of tears) and was concerned about the manner in which the Corinthians would respond to it. To Paul's joy and relief, the Corinthians responded with concern and love.

Paul recognizes that his letter caused some of them grief, but since it brought a change of heart to some, he was happy about the letter. He had no desire to hurt them, but he did want them to follow the message he taught them on an earlier visit. The sorrow experienced by the Corinthians came as a gift from God, leading them to spiritual growth. Sorrow that leads to spiritual growth leaves no grief behind. Paul admits he did not write the letter to hurt the one condemned or to hurt the community, but to bring about repentance. He expresses the comfort he found in their acceptance and change of heart.

Paul also rejoices because he has brought his friend Titus into contact with the people of Corinth. He writes that the spirit of Titus was refreshed by the Corinthians. He tells them that Titus loves them and was impressed by their obedience when they received him in fear. Their acceptance of Titus was so filled with love that Paul happily reports that they lived up to his boasting about them.

Review Questions

1. What does Paul mean when he says that now is the acceptable time?
2. What is involved in being called a people of God?
3. What does Paul mean when he speaks of making "holiness perfect in the fear of God"?
4. Why was Paul worried about the reaction of the Corinthian Christians to his letters?

Closing Prayer (SEE PAGE 18)

Pray the closing prayer now or after *lectio divina*.

Lectio Divina (SEE PAGE 11)

Relax your body and maintain a posture of prayer (back straight, eyes shut, feet flat on the floor). This exercise can take as long as you want, but in the context of this Bible study, 10 to 20 minutes should be sufficient.

The meditations that follow are provided only to help group participants use this prayer form, but note that *lectio* is intended to bring one to a place of prayerful contemplation where the Word of God speaks to the hearer from his or her heart. (See page 11 for further instruction.)

The acceptable time (6:1–13)

What makes Christians willing to dedicate themselves to Christ, even at difficult moments, expecting nothing in return? Paul lists all the difficulties he endures and those others must endure. Jesus has the answer when he urges his followers to store up treasures in heaven. He tells them, "For where your treasure is, there also will your heart be" (Matthew 6:21).

A very rich man lay dying in a hospital. During the last years of his life he battled diabetes, which led to a leg amputation. Years later he lay dying in the hospital, staring sullenly off into space and barking in anger at anyone who tried to offer a word of encouragement. He was angry because he knew he was dying and could do nothing about it. Because of his enormous wealth, he had grown accustomed to ordering others around. Now he was financially powerful, but he was a physically weak, dying man.

Shortly before he died, he remorsefully told his wife, "I'm a poor rich man, a prisoner tied to a hospital bed." He admitted his greatest pain was the realization that someone else would get his wealth and squander it. Since he knew that he had lived with no thought of God, he was frightened about what would happen to him after he died. This one-time powerful man died a sad death.

Contrary to the rich man who thought only of himself and lived a life of luxury, Paul accepted hardships because he made Jesus Christ and eternal life his treasure. The aim for all Christians is to meditate on the treasure that comes from Christ, and especially the treasure of a living faith in Christ. Paul, who was willing to endure all for the sake of Christ, was longing to go to the Lord. Christians who live a life faithful to Christ face death with greater acceptance than a rich person who never shared his or her wealth or gifts with others.

✠ *What can I learn from this passage?*

The temple of the living God (6:14—7:4)

Paul tells us that Christians are the temples of the living God. He adds that the temple of God has nothing to do with the temple of idols, which means that we must not open ourselves to sinful attitudes. In our world today, the idols come in the form of greed, immoral pleasure, popularity, or some worldly reward that drives a person to forget about God or to act as though God does not matter. For many, material goods matter more than God.

At a workshop about human nature, a woman spoke of the effects of television commercials on people. She said most people do not like to admit that they are trying to live the same lifestyle as their neighbor, but successful television commercials tell us otherwise. As an example, she referred to a commercial that showed a man washing his car and clearly envying the expensive car parked in the driveway next-door. In the next scene, the man who looked with envy is now pulling into his driveway with a car similar to that of his neighbor. The man, of course, has a broad smile on his face. She pointed out that the purpose of many commercials is to make a product an idol that people seek to possess.

As temples of God, Christians must act differently in the world that makes an idol out of products. Enjoying material goods is not evil, but Christians must challenge themselves to see if the idols of the world distract them from making Christ central to their lives.

✠ *What can I learn from this passage?*

Saddened into repentance (7:5–16)

Many people picture Paul as a dynamic person who feared nothing, yet when he expresses his feelings, he shows how thoroughly human he is. He tells the Corinthians that he had no rest and was afflicted with conflicts on the outside and fear on the inside. Paul loved the Corinthian Christians to the point of boasting about them to others.

Some reports about Archbishop Romero, a Catholic archbishop of San Salvador, tell us that he was often frightened when confronted with the idea that he might be assassinated, but he refused to allow his fear to dominate his life. Like many others who offered their lives for Christ and the poor, he believed that courage was not dying without fear, but living a faithful life despite fear. He was eventually assassinated for standing up against a regime that oppressed and killed many of the poor people of his country.

Like many saints, Paul experienced the human conditions of tiredness, external affliction, fear, joy, and a respectable pride. He shows the human emotions of missing someone and becoming discouraged. Paul suffered a great deal in spreading Christ's message, and he acted despite his fear. Christians may often have to act courageously for Christ and experience fear while doing so. Paul stands as an example of such courage and dedication.

✠ *What can I learn from this passage?*

PART 2: INDIVIDUAL STUDY (2 CORINTHIANS 8—9)

Day 1: Generosity in Giving (8:1–15)

Paul offers the Corinthians an example of overwhelming generosity as he points to the abundant gifts given by the Macedonians to the people of Jerusalem. A major theme of Paul's journeys is the collection for the poverty-stricken Christians of Jerusalem. Christianity had its origins in Jerusalem, and as a sign of the unity of all Christians with the Jerusalem church, a collection was taken up among the churches of Asia Minor and was brought to Jerusalem. Despite their own poverty and hardships, the Macedonians begged Paul to allow them to make an offering. Their overwhelming generosity showed their devotion to God and to Paul's call to help the people of Jerusalem. Titus, who has made a favorable beginning among the Corinthians, is sent by Paul to Corinth in an effort to get the Corinthians to share their gifts as the Macedonians had. Paul praises the Corinthians for the many gifts they have received from God, and he challenges them to add to these gifts the gift of charity. The collection has apparently already begun at Corinth, and Titus will bring it to its completion.

Paul makes it clear that he is not commanding the Corinthians to be generous in the collection but is instead hoping that they will act on their own with generosity. He reminds them of the gifts they have been given by Christ, who made himself poor that others might become rich in spiritual gifts. The example of the Macedonians and of Christ is offered to the Corinthians as a motivation for them to continue their generosity.

Paul adds a word of caution: The Corinthians should not give beyond their own needs, thereby leaving themselves in poverty. Instead, they should strive to offer the Jerusalem church a chance to live as they do, but they should not put themselves in poverty to allow others to do so. Their gifts at this time might gain not only a spiritual reward but also a reward in the future, when they could possibly find themselves in need. If this time should arrive, the Jerusalem church may be able to provide for them. Paul stresses the idea of living with equality, whereby all are able to live in the same manner because of the generosity of those who have a surplus.

As an example of God's providence and concern for equality, Paul quotes a verse from the Book of Exodus (16:18) that refers to the gathering of the manna in the desert. During the Exodus, the people were told to gather only a day's supply of manna. Some tried to gather more manna and found that they still ended up with the same amount as the others. Those who were not able to gather enough for their families found that they also had the same amount as the others. God enabled this Israelite equality.

Lectio Divina

Spend 8 to 10 minutes in silent contemplation of the following passage:

Paul asks but does not command the Corinthians to be generous. He is more interested in their attitude of trust than in their obedience to his commands. Obedience flows from trust in God. Paul, like many other saintly people, believes the gifts we receive are given for the common good. Jesus says, "Much will be required of the person entrusted with much, and still more will be demanded of the person entrusted with more" (Luke 12:48).

Saint John Neumann, a member of the Redemptorist Order and a former bishop of Philadelphia, traveled tirelessly for the sake of Christ's message and worked hard for the sake of Catholic education in his diocese. He is reported to have said that one can usually determine the dedication of a parishioner by his or her donation of time and treasure to God. John Neumann gave all he had for his service to God.

Paul has already spoken about the gifts of the Spirit, and he now speaks about monetary gifts. He is addressing the total life of the Corinthians. Every gift we have comes from God and is given to us for the common good. Jesus expects more from those who receive more. This includes every type of gift, including time, talent, and treasure.

✠ *What can I learn from this passage?*

Day 2: Paul and Titus Send Apostles (8:16–24)

Paul states that God has blessed Titus with a great concern for the Corinthians. Titus already showed a deep generosity by freely volunteering to go to Corinth to pick up the collection and bring it to Jerusalem. Along with Titus, Paul sends a second one he refers to as a "brother" who has received praise in all the churches for his preaching of the gospel. Though Paul does not name this brother, he is apparently someone well known to the Corinthians. The churches have appointed this "brother" to travel with Paul for the collection that Paul is administrating for the sake of the Lord.

Paul states that he wishes to avoid any false accusations concerning his handling of the collection, so he does not touch it himself. His fears may stem from the problems already faced with the Corinthian church, which has accused him of other misdeeds in the past. He does not wish false accusations to hinder his ministry of spreading the gospel. Rather than prove himself to any human judge, Paul seeks only God's approval.

He states that he is also sending another brother (a third one), who has apparently endured some of the afflictions experienced by Paul and proved himself. Paul adds him to the group because of his confidence in the Corinthians. He again does not identify this brother to the reader, apparently because he also is well known to the Corinthians and Paul feels no need to name him. Titus receives special praise as Paul's partner and coworker. The brothers, through their ministry, are considered apostles of the churches who express by their lives the glory of Christ. Paul recommends these three brothers to the Corinthians, urging them to prove by their love that he does not boast in vain about the Christians of Corinth.

Lectio Divina

Spend 8 to 10 minutes in silent contemplation of the following passage:

The word *apostle* means "one who is sent." Because Jesus sent out his twelve close companions, we call them apostles—the first to be sent by Christ. Paul rightly addresses those he sends to Corinth as apostles because they were "sent." Each baptized Christian is sent by Christ to share with others the gifts God has given us. In this way, we can say that every Christian is an apostle.

A high school senior, whose mother had raised him since her divorce from her husband seven years earlier, decided to visit his father's mother, whom he hadn't heard from since his parents' divorce. His desire to visit with her had been nagging him for more than a month, but he kept ignoring it. Now, although she lived four hours away, he decided to take a bus to visit her. Since his memories of her were vague, he felt a telephone call would not work; he wanted to see her face to face.

Upon his arrival, she opened the door and he said with a smile, "Hi, Grandma." She looked startled, and then, grabbing and hugging him, she began to sob like a baby. "I've been so depressed," she said. "I thought I'd never hear from you again." Later, over a quickly prepared meal, she said, "I've prayed so hard to see you again. I think God sent you."

Whenever we perform some good deed in life, we may overlook the fact that God may have sent us to the person who needed our help. Jesus said, "It was not you who chose me, but I who chose you and appointed you to go and bear fruit that will remain" (John 15:16). Just as Paul sent out his companions, Christ, through the action of the Spirit in our lives, has chosen us and sent us into the world with the gift of faith and talents to be used with that gift.

✠ *What can I learn from this passage?*

Day 3: God's Indescribable Gift (9:1–15)

The letter of recommendation to Achaia seems to be another in this collection of letters that makes up 2 Corinthians. Corinth is the capital of Achaia. Just as Paul boasted to the Corinthians about the generosity of the Macedonians, he now acknowledges that he has boasted in the same way about the Corinthians when speaking to the Macedonians. His boasting about the Corinthians motivated the Macedonians to make a generous offering. Paul asks the Corinthians to have their generous gifts ready lest some Macedonians come with him and find—to Paul's embarrassment and the embarrassment of the Corinthians—that his boasting was in vain. He is sending some of his companions ahead to gather the collection and to have it ready. Paul reminds them again that the offering should be freely given and not considered a burden.

Paul uses a text from the Book of Proverbs (11:24) that proclaims the generous grow richer while those who lack generosity lose what they have. He compares generosity to a seed that is sown. A sparse sowing leads to a sparse harvest, and a generous sowing leads to a generous harvest. Just as the generous person shows confidence in God's generosity, each one must give joyfully and not grudgingly. Paul quotes from Psalm 112:9 when he relates how God provides for the poor throughout all ages. God, from whom every seed and bread comes, provides an abundant growth for the generous donor. God provides the seed that is planted and the wheat that is harvested. The donor receives a double gift, namely, the joy of providing for another in need and the grateful favor that comes from God.

Although Paul does not name the recipients of this collection, we know it is for the people of Jerusalem. Some people of Jerusalem had doubts about Paul's ministry to the Gentiles, but Paul now tells the Corinthians that their generosity will lead the members of the Jerusalem church to praise God for them. These members will also be praying for the church at Corinth. Paul closes this passage by thanking God for this overwhelming gift.

Lectio Divina

Spend 8 to 10 minutes in silent contemplation of the following passage:

Paul's thoughts offer a means to happiness. He is saying that God rewards those who use their gifts well. It does not mean God will give us a large sum of money if we donate a large sum to someone, but it may mean that other gifts, such as the experience of joy and gratitude, could result from our offering. The giving person often finds contentment and happiness in life.

When someone asked the owner of a bookstore what books sell the most, he gave a surprising answer. He said that after the Bible, the books about achieving happiness and success sold the most. People are always looking for ways to achieve happiness, and a surprising number of books have been written on the subject.

Christians, however, find that the real road to happiness comes in knowing, loving, and serving God. The Bible is the most informative book on achieving happiness because it teaches a motivation for living life and an example of living faithfully in God's service. Sharing our gifts will not free us from the daily difficulties of life, but this action will enable us to approach them with a contentment that comes from knowing that one is doing what God wishes. Jesus said, "For the measure with which you measure will in return be measured out to you" (Luke 6:38). What we give freely comes back to us in some manner.

✠ *What can I learn from this passage?*

Review Questions

1. Why is Paul so concerned about the church of God in Jerusalem?

2. What can Paul's approach to the collection for the church teach us today?

3. Why is the generosity in giving to the collection for Jerusalem an important part of Paul's boasting about the Corinthians?

4. How does the expression, "We reap what we sow," apply to Paul's message to the Corinthians?

Boasting in the Lord

2 CORINTHIANS 10—13

For it is not the one who recommends himself who is approved, but the one whom the Lord recommends (10:18).

Opening Prayer (SEE PAGE 18)

Context

Part 1: 2 Corinthians 10—11:29 Some accuse Paul of being harsh in his letters and weak when he visits them. Paul recalls for the Corinthians that authority was given to him in Christ for building them up, not for tearing them down. He does not compare himself to others, but accepts that his boasting, if any, should be done in the Lord. All he has and does comes from the Lord. He preaches among them without asking any recompense for his ministry. He does this so that no one can say anything against him concerning rewards for his mission, and he also preaches freely because he loves them. Paul offers a strange type of boasting when he boasts of being an Israelite to confront those who claim to be better Israelites than he. He also boasts of his beatings, sufferings, dangers, and hunger. These events show how weak he is, yet they are also signs of his power.

Part 2: 2 Corinthians 11:30—13 Paul continues to boast about his weaknesses. He was humiliated when he had to be lowered in a basket through a window in the fortress wall to escape capture. He can also boast of a vision he had that he cannot fully explain, except that he believes he was caught up somehow in paradise, and he speaks of the event as though he were speaking of someone else experiencing this. He suffered from some physical malady that he prayed God would heal, but God did not heal him. He sees this as a gift from God that keeps him from being proud. He claims he is not inferior to the so-called "superapostles," reminding the Corinthians that he dedicated himself to them as other apostles dedicated themselves to their ministry. Also, he warns the Corinthians that he is about to visit them for a third time and hopes he can come in love and harmony and not have to reprimand them. He ends by blessing them in the name of the Trinity.

PART 1: GROUP STUDY (2 CORINTHIANS 10—11:29)

Read aloud 2 Corinthians 10—11:29.

10:1–18 Paul's boast

Paul's letter of tears begins with this passage. He tells his listeners that he follows the meekness and gentleness of Christ in addressing them, but some of the Corinthians apparently misunderstand Paul. They claim he is weak while in their midst but bold when away from them. Paul hopes he will not have to act with boldness, proclaiming he has powerful spiritual weapons to use against his accusers. In this passage he again uses the imagery of a soldier in battle. His power is the power of God, which destroys every false wisdom and pretention that militates against God's power. He sees himself as a triumphant soldier who captures everything for Christ. Once the Corinthians have accepted Christ, Paul is ready to speak out against those who are disobedient to this call.

Paul accuses the Corinthians of interpreting things in a shallow manner. For those who claim to have a special relationship with Christ, Paul tells them that he belongs to Christ as much as they do. Now that he has begun to boast about the good works he performed among them, he will not be ashamed to continue if it leads to the strengthening of their faith. He tells them he does not wish to intimidate them with his letters, referring to some letters written in the past to the community. Some of these letters may likely be contained in earlier parts of this Second Letter to the Corinthians, and some others may have been lost. The Corinthians accuse Paul of having strong words in his letters and weak speech when in their midst, so he warns that he will be as forceful and strong when he is with them as he is in his letters.

Some other preachers have apparently set up certain norms with which to compare their successes. These norms, however, actually show that these preachers are ignorant of their true mission. Paul refuses to use these norms to compare himself with others. Instead he uses the norms set up by God. He believes he has the right to speak to the Corinthians in a strong manner, since he is the founder of the church at Corinth. He recognizes the work of others in the Corinthian community, and he will not claim any credit for it. He does hope that their faith will grow as they reflect on the gospel he preaches and that this faith will affect them to the degree that they themselves will evangelize. He intends to preach elsewhere, but he does not intend to take credit for the ministry of others in these territories.

Paul repeats a message found earlier in his First Letter to the Corinthians (1:31). If anyone feels the need to boast, he or she should boast about the work the Lord is performing in their midst. Those who commend themselves gain nothing, but those whom the Lord commends are truly acceptable.

11:1–15 Preaching without charge

Despite Paul's directions to the Corinthians that they ignore the boasting of others, Paul is now willing to become foolish enough to boast about himself, while begging the Corinthians to tolerate his boasting. In reality, his boast becomes a boast about the Lord. The Scriptures often speak of God's jealousy when the people of God choose other false gods. It is this jealousy that God has for "the Chosen" that underlies Paul's actions. In founding the church at Corinth, Paul has given the Corinthians to God as a chaste bride to a husband. Paul recalls how the serpent seduced Eve (Genesis 3:1–6), and he fears the people of Corinth might be seduced by this same evil serpent. The source of his fear lies in the Corinthians' love of prestige and novelty, and Paul fears they will be overcome by a new type of preaching or a new gospel. He boasts that he is not inferior to any of the so-called "superapostles," whom he refers to as "false" apostles a few verses later (11:13). These "superapostles" seem to be those with great eloquence and pompous wisdom. Paul admits that he may lack their eloquence, but he refuses to accept any accusation that he is inferior to them in knowledge. He calls on the Corinthians to witness to this themselves by looking at what he has already done in their midst.

Some have apparently accused Paul of not acting as a true apostle because he did not allow the Corinthians to support him in his ministry. He nevertheless refuses to change his tactics. He states that he "robbed" other churches, meaning he took alms from these other churches, although they had no obligation to support his ministry among the Corinthians. Paul accepted this support from some of the Macedonians so that the Corinthians could not refuse his ministry on the grounds that it was too great a material burden.

Paul challenges the claims of those who look for material support in the ministry by not allowing them to point to him as an example of their right to this support. He calls these others "false apostles" and implies that they are agents of the devil. Even Satan would act in an angelic way to deceive others and make them turn away from Christ. Paul, therefore, is not surprised that these false preachers disguise themselves as ministers of righteousness. He declares that they will receive what they deserve.

11:16–29 Paul boasts of his labors and suffering

Because the Corinthians admire those who boast, Paul is willing to become a fool for them and take his turn at boasting as well. He admits this is not the way the Lord would have it, but he does this for the sake of the Corinthians and chides them for their false wisdom. He calls himself a fool by their standards. In their wisdom, Paul tells them, they will certainly tolerate a fool. They are willing to accept those who take advantage of them, those who act as though they have great wisdom, and those who punish them. Paul admits he does not have the strength to do such things. He calls himself too "weak" to act in this manner.

He then challenges the false preachers to match their credentials with his. Like them, he is a Hebrew, an Israelite, a true son of Abraham. In his foolishness, Paul goes even further when he claims he is more a minister of Christ than they are. He has suffered imprisonment, beatings, and near-death situations. He has been whipped five times by the Jews, three times by pagans, stoned once, shipwrecked three times, and left on the sea for a full day. Some of these events are verified by the accounts found in the Acts of the Apostles, but some are not found anywhere else except here in Paul's own words. In spreading the message, he suffered everything from natural disasters to human conflict. He also endured mental anguish for the churches he established on his journeys.

Review Questions

1. Why does Paul try to avoid being harsh with the Corinthians when he visits them?

2. How might we understand Paul's teaching on boasting? What does Paul teach us about comparing ourselves to others?

3. What does Paul mean when he says we should boast in the Lord? What does Paul wish to prove by boasting about his sufferings?

4. Is it significant that Paul preaches to the Corinthians free of charge? Explain and share.

Closing Prayer (SEE PAGE 18)

Pray the closing prayer now or after *lectio divina*.

Lectio Divina (SEE PAGE 11)

Relax your body and maintain a posture of prayer (back straight, eyes shut, feet flat on the floor). This exercise can take as long as you want, but in the context of this Bible study, 10 to 20 minutes should be sufficient.

The meditations that follow are provided only to help group participants use this prayer form, but note that *lectio* is intended to bring one to a place of prayerful contemplation where the Word of God speaks to the hearer from his or her heart. (See page 11 for further instruction.)

Paul's boast (10:1–18)

Saint Teresa of Avila once said that humility is truth. Paul boasts in the Lord, aware that the gifts he has come from God. He notes how foolish it is to boast of something he has not accomplished. In a sense, we can say

Paul's boast is that he recognizes the foolishness of boasting. Boasting often comes from people who are weak, insecure, and in need of praise for their accomplishments.

A man saved a three-year-old boy who fell from a second-story window by catching the boy in his arms before the boy hit the ground. The town television station featured the hero and interviewed him on the air. When they asked what made him take a chance on saving the boy, he began to boast that he was very athletic and that it was easy for him to catch the boy. He continued to talk about his athletic abilities to the point that most people who previously admired him now found him to be an egotistical bore. After the program, the station received an influx of negative twitters saying that the viewers disliked the man. He defeated himself by bragging about how good he was.

Since humility is truth, Paul can recognize that he has received great gifts, but he always gives credit to the Lord working through him. We all have spiritual and physical gifts given us by God. We can boast about having these gifts, but we must always remember that God has given them to us. Our boasting should always glorify the Lord.

✠ *What can I learn from this passage?*

Preaching without charge (11:1–15)

In this passage, Paul claims he lacked the ability to preach like others, but he also realized that God bestowed on him a special knowledge. He admitted he had this gift, but he did not make it a reason for boasting. He realized that all the knowledge in the world does not make people more spiritual. God was the one who worked this miracle.

A pastor had the reputation of being an excellent preacher, and he prayed each day that the Holy Spirit would allow his words to touch the hearts of those to whom he was preaching. He was wise enough to know that it was not his skill in preaching that helped people draw closer to the Lord, but the power of God. He knew that if anyone became more prayerful or saintly because of his preaching, it was the work of the Lord. His aim was not to be an entertainer, but a preacher who touched the hearts of his listeners.

Paul, like that pastor, was a realist. He was an instrument of the Lord. It was up to the Lord to make his words touch someone's heart. Christians who wish to touch the hearts of others and bring them closer to God must realize that the gifts they possess and use come from God and are given for the common good. Gifts, humility, and prayer enable us to touch the lives of others.

✠ *What can I learn from this passage?*

Paul boasts of his labors and suffering (11:16–29)

A common expression states that a person not only talks the talk but walks the walk. This means that people do not simply preach about something but that they prove the truth of what they are saying by showing they are willing to live what they preach.

Saint John Bosco is a perfect example of one who not only talked the talk but walked the walk. He worked tirelessly for street children and delinquents. It is reported that he went into a saloon begging for funds for the children. A man at the bar spit in his face when he approached him. John Bosco said, "That was for me. Now would you help my children?"

Paul talked about Christ and his message, and he walked the walk by accepting beatings, insults, and near-death situations for the sake of Christ. People like Paul and John Bosco never knew what dangers and humiliations they would endure each day, but they trusted the Lord to be their companion and strength in all their endeavors.

✠ *What can I learn from this passage?*

PART 2: INDIVIDUAL STUDY (2 CORINTHIANS 11:30—13)

Day 1: Paul Boasts of Visions and Encouragement (11:30—12:10)

God knows how Paul suffered with the weakness of each member and the scandal that some endured. Paul adds that he was lowered in a basket from a window in the wall at Damascus. Some see this last event as a humiliation for Paul, yet he adds it to this list to show how foolish he is willing to become for Christ.

Paul's foolishness leads him to boast about his visions and revelations, something that would be most impressive to the Corinthians who held mystical experiences in such high esteem. He speaks to them of a vision he has kept secret until now, a vision that occurred fourteen years earlier. In describing this vision, Paul speaks of himself in the third person, possibly due to his experience of being outside of himself during the vision. He implies he had nothing to do with the experience when he says he was "caught up into paradise." He could not put his experience into words, either because he was not allowed to report the exact experience or, more likely, because human words could not describe the event. Paul says he can boast about "such a one" because it was not something he did but something that was done to him.

When it comes to his own doing, Paul can boast only of his weakness. Paul refrains from boasting lest others think he is greater than he really is. He tells the Corinthians that he also received some type of "thorn in the flesh" to prevent him from becoming conceited. The thorn in the flesh that keeps him humble is never identified, but it appears to be some type of physical ailment. Like Christ during his agony in the Garden of Gethsemane, Paul three times begged God to take this thorn away from him, but he was told instead that God's grace was sufficient for him. A continual theme of Paul's writings is that power comes from weakness. He tells the Corinthians that this is the message he received from the Lord, that power reaches its perfection in weakness. Paul realizes his strength comes from Christ and not from himself, and his weakness makes the power of Christ more easily recognized. He accepts every type of weakness, since his powerlessness makes him strong in Christ.

Lectio Divina

Spend 8 to 10 minutes in silent contemplation of the following passage:

In the Gospel of Matthew (17:1–8), we read that Jesus was transfigured in the presence of his disciples. As they came down the mountain, the disciples must certainly have had a different image of Jesus.

A devout woman had a near-death experience during an operation. For a moment, the doctors thought she'd died when she stopped breathing, but she began to breathe again. The woman told of seeing her deceased relatives and the overwhelming peace and joy she felt.

She later told her husband, "It was wonderful. I don't fear death anymore. In fact, I think I welcome it."

Paul describes an experience of being out of his body and surrounded by unimaginable peace and beauty. We have not enjoyed an experience of being in some type of heavenly presence, but through faith, we view the world differently than those without faith. After Jesus' resurrection, he appeared to his disciples and said to Thomas, "Blessed are those who have not seen and have believed" (John 20:29). Through faith, Christians are lifted out of the everyday experiences of life and are able to declare that there is more to life than that which is known, felt, or seen by the senses. The world is transfigured in the eyes of Christians through faith.

✠ *What can I learn from this passage?*

Day 2: Paul's Concern for the Church at Corinth (12:11–21)

Because the Corinthians did not defend Paul and his good work among them, Paul complains that they have driven him to play the role of a fool who must boast about himself. He admits he is nothing, but he does not accept any accusation that would make him less than the so-called "superapostles." Some have apparently hinted that Paul was not a true apostle. Paul points to the powerful deeds he performed in their midst as a sign of his apostleship. Others have apparently expressed shame about Paul's acceptance of support from others rather than from them. Paul first apologizes for this, but then declares that he intends to continue the practice. Just as a parent does not seek any support from his or her children but must support the children, so Paul will not seek any support from them. The children (the Corinthians) cannot claim that Paul owes them anything.

Others have apparently accused Paul of tricking them and misusing the collection. He names those sent to take the collection and challenges the Corinthians to accuse them of the same deceitfulness. If they accuse Paul of taking advantage of them, then they must also accuse Titus, whom they love, of taking advantage of them. Since Titus was sent by Paul, he would have had to have some part in the deception if it were true.

Paul declares he does not write in this vein to defend himself but to build up the community. He fears that he will find some vices still existing among them and that he will react with anger. He will not be happy with the sins of the Corinthians, and they will not be happy with his *angry* response to their sinfulness. The Corinthians have come to Christ from paganism, and Paul fears he will find some of their sinfulness still being practiced. The result will be that everyone, the Corinthians as well as Paul, will be humiliated by the outburst that will follow. In the Gospel of Matthew, the author has Christ proclaim, "Blessed are they who mourn, for they will be comforted" (5:4). The mourning referred to in the gospel is one's mourning over sinfulness. Paul declares he will mourn in this manner when he finds his beloved Corinthians still engaged in the sinful deeds he condemned on a previous visit.

Lectio Divina

Spend 8 to 10 minutes in silent contemplation of the following passage:

After preaching about the love of Christ to the Corinthians, Paul still finds some who attempt to reject or humiliate him. He came to them performing good deeds, and some forced him to defend himself against their false accusations.

An elderly woman who lived alone could no longer care for the property around her house. A neighbor would mow her lawn for her during the summer and shovel her walks in the winter, never allowing her to pay him for his work. When others in the neighborhood saw this, some said he was helping the woman, who was quite wealthy, because he hoped she would leave him her wealth. The man, however, already knew she intended to give her wealth to her nephews and nieces who lived a distance away and who occasionally visited her and phoned her often.

Jesus is a loving God. Yet despite his obvious concern for others, some jealous religious leaders began to accuse him of being not only a devil but the prince of devils. Christians who follow Christ can expect to be rejected, just as he was. Being a good person does not always mean other people are willing to recognize goodness. Paul was a good person, dedicated to the people of Jerusalem and Corinth, but he had to endure criticism for his good works. The criticism, however, did not deter him from his mission.

✠ *What can I learn from this passage?*

Day 3: Paul Challenges the Church at Corinth (13:1–13)

Paul quotes from the Book of Deuteronomy (19:15), which speaks of an accusation being established on the evidence of two or three witnesses. He views his next visit to the Corinthians (his third) as his final indictment against them. If they are still in sin at that time, he will speak out with the authority of Christ, who is not weak in dealing with them. In his death, Christ confirmed his weakness, but through his resurrection, he demonstrated the power of God. In the same way, all Christians share in the weakness and power of Christ.

Several times in this letter to the Christians at Corinth, Paul had to defend himself against their accusations. He now challenges them to examine themselves to see if they have lived up to their faith and the message of the gospel. He asks whether they truly realize that Christ is in them. He prays that they have done no wrong, not for his sake, but for theirs. Even if he appeared to them to fail at times, he hopes they will have received a favorable outcome. He tells them he can only do what he believes is the truth. He is so concerned for the church at Corinth that he can rejoice when they appear strong, even if he appears weak. And he declares he comes to them with the authority of Christ.

Paul explains that he is writing his letter in a harsh manner so that he does not have to confront them with such harshness when he arrives among them. His mission is to build up the community, not to tear it down, and he does not wish to cause any tensions when he visits them. He realizes he has authority since he is acting in the name of Christ. Although he does not mention it, Paul may also be acting with such authority as the original apostle and initiator of the church of God at Corinth.

Ending abruptly, Paul tells the Corinthians to rejoice and exhorts them to change their ways by encouraging one another. He further calls them to live in harmony and peace that the God of love and peace may be with them. He also tells them to greet one another with a *holy kiss*. This is equivalent to our kiss of peace at the Eucharist. He sends greetings from the holy ones, who in this case are most likely the Macedonian Christians. The term *holy ones* in Paul's era designated the followers of Christ. Paul ends with a blessing that clearly expresses his faith in the Trinity. He ordinarily ends with some blessing from God through Christ, but the emphasis placed on the gifts of the Spirit in the Corinthian community makes the blessing in the name of the Lord Jesus Christ, God, and the Holy Spirit most appropriate.

Lectio Divina

Spend 8 to 10 minutes in silent contemplation of the following passage:

Someone once said, "I would rather be respected than loved, although I would like to have both." Paul is hoping to come to the Corinthians in peace and harmony rather than coming to discipline or reprimand them. He has a deep love and respect for them, and he prays he will not discourage them when he must reprimand them. Although it would be unpleasant for him to be harsh with the Christians of Corinth, he is willing to do so for their sake and the sake of Christ.

Parents realize they must reprimand their children when the children do something that may hurt themselves or another. Parents have a right to seek respect from their children, but parents also realize they discipline their children because they love them. They know that true discipline must be enacted with love and respect for the child, always avoiding any emotional or physical injury to the child.

In the daily events of life, Christians often face situations in which they must opt to seek respect rather than love, especially in cases in which they reject joining others in sin. Paul has the opportunity to gain the love of the sinners in the Corinthian community, but he warns them that they might not find him as friendly as they wish. He comes to them as a parent to children, praising them for their good deeds and scolding them for their misdeeds. As a follower of Christ, Paul acknowledges that his message may at times gain the respect of others without gaining their love.

✠ *What can I learn from this passage?*

Review Questions

1. Since Paul boasts of his good deeds, does that mean that we, too, should boast of our good deeds?

2. How do our weaknesses help us to trust God's presence in our lives?

3. What can we learn from Paul's dedication to the church of God at Corinth?

4. What does Paul mean when he tells the Corinthians that he hopes they will bring to completeness what he has already begun in them?

About the Author

William A. Anderson, DMin, PhD, is a presbyter of the Diocese of Wheeling-Charleston in West Virginia. This director of retreats and parish missions, professor, catechist, spiritual director, and former pastor has written extensively on pastoral, spiritual, and religious subjects. Father Anderson earned his doctor of ministry degree from St. Mary's Seminary & University in Baltimore and his doctorate in sacred theology from Duquesne University in Pittsburgh.